DARE

TO BE

AVERAGE

Also by David Martin

MY FRIEND W   -   Arriviste Press 2005

DARE TO BE AVERAGE

A collection of essays to help you lead an ordinary life.

DAVID MARTIN

Copyright 2010 by David Martin

All rights reserved. No part of this book may be reproduced or transmitted in any form or by any means, electronic or mechanical, including photocopying, recording, digitizing, or by any information storage and retrieval system, without permission from the author.

The selections in this book were previously published as indicated at the beginning of each selection.

ISBN 978-0-557-44481-6

CONTENTS

Introduction..ix

CHAPTER ONE - WORK

Build Your Own Job..2
Bureaucraticide..4
Cubicle, Sweet Cubicle...6
Bob Moore..8
A Lesson in Bureaucracy..10
Nice Work if You Can Get It..12
A Death by E-mail Misadventure..14

CHAPTER TWO - HOME REPAIR

I've Got a Handle on This..19
Dude Where's My Rec Room?...21
Product Requires Assembly...23
Must-have Tools for the Not-so Handyman............................26
Fences? Hard Work Makes Good Neighbors..........................28
Appliance Apocalypse Now..30
When Bad Cars Happen to Good People................................32
My Autoerotic Affair..34
Poof Goes the Lightbulb...36
The Time and Skills Required of a Real Man.........................38

v

CHAPTER THREE - PARENTING

A Toddler's Handbook for Parentcare..41
A Toddler's Guide to Toilet Training..43
A Toddler's Guide to Summer Vacation..45
Whose Birthday is It Anyway? 47
The Cruel Kindness of Mistress Sarah..49
Parenting Quiz Stumps This Dad..51
Apocalypse This Week: Diary of a Parent Survivor...........................53
Whatever You Do, Parents, Do Not Follow This Advice...................56
Dueling Over Diapers..58

CHAPTER FOUR - FINANCES

Just Zig When I Zag..62
Have You Really Made It? 64
The Dialectic of Garage Sales...66
Tax, Where is Thy Sting? 69
Fund, Fund, Fund...72
How I Became a Believer..74

CHAPTER FIVE - RELATIONSHIPS

Breakfast and a Movie...78
Beware the Stepford Husband..81
29 Ways to Know He's Not Cheating..84
Romancing the Stoned...86
To Sleep, Perchance to Dream...89
Dog Days..91
The Kama Sutra of Housework..94
Husband Instruction Manual..96

CHAPTER SIX - VACATIONS

The Diary of a Winter Getaway..99
A Week in the Cottage..102
A Timeshare Romance..105
Family Camp 17..107
Do Come to Our Cottage..109

CHAPTER SEVEN - HEALTH, DIET & EXERCISE

Sweet Dreams, the Twinkies Diet..112
Nasty, Brutish and Short...114
All This Exercising..116
Avoiding Caffeine?...118
One Way to Quit Smoking...120
Scratching a 49-year Old Itch..123

CHAPTER EIGHT - AGING

A Manly Mid-life Day..126
Martin v. Father Time..128
My Numbers Are Up...130
You're Not Getting Older..132
Life After 50 134
Who's on First? 136
Are You There God? 138

CHAPTER NINE - DARE TO BE AVERAGE

Dare to Be Average...141

Seven Habits of Unmotivated People..144
Seven Steps to Average..146
I'd Like to Volunteer..148
You Have One Minute, 28 Seconds..150
Recycling for Dummies..152
Could You Leave Me a Note? 154
A Membership Drive for the Latter Day Daves............................156
A Night Out at the Movies...157
Dave's Law..159

INTRODUCTION

What do you do with twenty years' worth of published humor pieces? Well, if you're Dave Barry or Dwight David Eisenhower, you're famous enough that some big publisher will come calling and pay you to put them all in a nice big book.

Like Ike and Dave Barry, I am named David but unfortunately the similarities end there. So instead of waiting for some big publisher to print my output from the last two decades, I decided to do it myself.

"Dare to be Average" is the result of my efforts to gather my works into one small volume. I'd like to say that I spent untold hours compiling, editing and arranging my various essays but that would be a lie.

Instead, I quickly categorized them under nine chapter headings and that was that. The pieces have previously appeared in publications such as *The New York Times, The Chicago Tribune, The Christian Science Monitor* and *The Smithsonian Magazine*. I hope you enjoy the collection and that it will help you to stop aiming for the stars and inspire you instead to truly "dare to be average."

- David Martin

CHAPTER ONE

WORK

"Build Your Own Job"
The New York Times   January 21, 1999

I recently read a psychological profile of Independent Prosecutor Ken Starr written by a Professor Aubrey Immelman. I found the profile interesting. But even more interesting was Professor Immelman's title - political psychologist.

This was a new concept to me. I knew what a psychologist was and I knew what a politician was. But I had never before heard of a political psychologist.

After some thought, it occurred to me that Professor Immelman may be on to something. By cross-fertilizing professions, he has come up with a whole new occupational group.

But why stop with political psychologist? With a little imagination, anyone should be able to marry two disparate fields into a new job. Just take your pick from one of these up and coming professions:

Social economist
You're giving a dinner party and you need entertainment. Who do you call? A social economist - that's who. He'll regale your guests with fascinating stories of supply and demand curves, monetary policy and the history of the Federal Reserve Board.

Recreational physicist
Unsure of the correct propane setting on your barbecue? Can't seem to get the hang of the aerodynamics of the Frisbee? Call on the recreational physicist. He can assess the mechanics, optics or thermodynamics of any outdoor activity and get you back on the fun track.

Legal engineer
When you're in a legal dilemma and you're surrounded by hostile statutes and regulations, call for a legal engineer. She can dismantle that nasty legislation and rebuild it to suit your particular fact situation.

Metaphysical plumber
Having some doubts about where you came from and where you're going? Sensing some leaks in the cosmos? The metaphysical plumber can set things right. Using his philosopher's snake, he can clean the doubts from your existential pipes and help you to achieve a new cosmic flow.

Ethical dentist
    She's the one you call when you need to be extracted from one of those tricky moral dilemmas or you need a nasty spiritual cavity filled. If necessary, she can even perform restoration work on everything from core beliefs to root causes.
    If none of these new occupations appeals to you, create your own. All you need is one of my new job generators like the one shown below. Pick a word from column A and one from column B and you've got yourself a new profession.

Column A	Column B
musical	philosopher
chemical	historian
domestic	painter
surgical	florist
sociological	lawyer

    Try it, just for fun. Take the first one from column A and the last one from column B. What have you got? A musical lawyer.
    What does that mean? I don't know and neither does anyone else. So you're free to make it up as you go. He's a lawyer who sings his submissions in court. Or he's someone who analyzes the legal ramifications of song. Or he's a pianist who only uses the gray keys.
    The beauty of your new job is that you decide. By choosing one from column A and one from column B, you've just created a career that didn't exist before. If you decide what it means, who's to say you're wrong?
    This is great news for the economy. Unemployed, downsized or just bored? Use one of my job generators and you're back in business. In fact, I think I've just found a new profession for myself - occupational builder.

"Bureaucraticide"
Stitches Magazine   November, 1997

I love being a bureaucrat. The soft shuffle of paper on a crisp spring morning. The low whir of red tape endlessly unwinding. The irate screams of someone being given the telephone runaround. These are the sweet sounds of obstruction that are music to my ears.

But not everyone revels in the torpor of government. Some yearn for so-called meaningful work. Others long for a workplace free from endless rules and regulations. Many feel trapped in a world not of their own making.

What to do with the poor souls who have reached the end of their collective rope? They're too young to retire and too old to ever hope to return to the outside world. There's only one realistic solution - death with dignity.

Office suicide is the answer. Yes - when there's nowhere else to go, it's time to turn out the lights and head to the great paper shredder in the sky.

And what better way to go than in the line of duty. Face down on the desk, out for the count, functionaries will have the satisfaction of knowing that someone they love will be happily spending all those death benefits. And by expiring on the job, they'll also help to keep other bureaucrats employed in processing the endless paperwork their deaths will create. But how best to make the parting as painless as possible? Bureaucrats are not violent people. They're not likely to off themselves by exiting a window headfirst, driving themselves face first onto a thumbtack covered desk or even inflicting a series of paper cuts. Much too painful; much too messy.

No, the most suitable way to go is to slowly paint one's entire body with that hideous white correction fluid. The bureaucrat covered in White-Out, Snopaque or any of the dozen other brands of white goop will just slowly suffocate to death.

Another way out is to stop pushing paper. The only thing keeping most bureaucrats from death is the constant movement of all those files, memos and reports. Stop sending them on and before you know it you've created your own paper tomb.

Some may wish to opt for a more traditional approach. The

telephone cord strangulation method is a time tested, effective technique. Performing this one during the middle of an actual call adds a nice dramatic touch.

My personal choice for office hara-kiri is in step with the latest in technology. Turn on your personal computer and strap your face to the CRT screen. This method has advantages over the old strap your face to the photocopier technique. First, you give the appearance that you're still working. And second, you don't have to keep pressing the start button.

A relatively quick method is to short circuit your dictating machine. This one works best while standing in a pool of water. A suitable alternative is to pour your coffee over the microphone. You may even want to leave a tape running in the machine to record your departing words.

The choices are endless. You could slowly poison yourself with a daily dose of duplicating fluid from the photocopier. Placing one's tie in an electric typewriter is always popular. And paper shredders open up a whole new world of possibilities.

Perhaps the surest and most effective method is to simply introduce interesting work without warning. Heart failure is almost guaranteed. If this method fails, check to see if the individual was alive in the first place.

So, if you're a bureaucrat and you feel the malaise descending upon you, don't wait for retirement - go now. This is one area where you can show some initiative. Otherwise you may be facing a new government program - on the job euthanasia.

"Cubicle, Sweet Cubicle"
The Ottawa Citizen   August 19, 2002

Feng shui is the ancient Chinese art of aligning and arranging your living quarters to ensure a proper flow of the life force *chi*. It involves the harmonization of the elements in your home to obtain a healthy balance in your life.

For example, if your bathroom is in the centre of your house, that's bad *feng shui* because that's the wealth area: The frequent flow of water is flushing potential wealth down the drain.

There seems to be a lot written about the art of *feng shui* for the home. There are even books providing information on *feng shui* for office buildings and executive suites. But there's not a lot written about harmonizing the work space of the modern employee: the cubicle. And that, of course, is where I come in. After exhaustive research and painstaking trial-and-error experimentation, I have become a *feng shui* master of the workstation.

First, you must ensure that the negative events of the past that still inhabit your cubicle are eliminated. For example, your predecessor may have committed bureaucraticide by covering his entire body in White-Out or Snopaque. Or the previous occupant may have received a pink slip. No problem.

The solution is to perform a cleansing ceremony which will banish the negative forces from the past that are still lurking about. This involves placing high-level memos over the floor, sprinkling dust obtained from an enclosed executive office and chanting the sacred words "early retirement, early retirement" over and over.

Once you've cleansed your cubicle, it's time to get to work on rearranging its contents. It makes sense, of course, that it's good *feng shui* to have your desk facing the window. This gives you something to do in the afternoon.

Unfortunately, facing the window usually means your back is to the door. So, in order to achieve proper balance (and not be caught napping), it's necessary to place a mirror in front of your desk. Alternatively, wind chimes can be hung at your cubicle entrance to warn you of intruders. Or you can simply place upturned thumbtacks on your desk to guarantee alertness.

It's good cubicle *feng shui* to be surrounded by your office furniture -- this protects you from the evil spirit irate client who may want to wring your neck. A furniture fortress will give you a fighting chance against such interlopers. If possible, build an escape route into your plan.

A computer means bad *feng shui*. It's going to malfunction and there's not much you can do about it. If you must have a computer in your office, place it as far away from your desk as possible. A computer's ability to work properly is directly proportional to its distance from the user.

Bare cubicle walls are bad *feng shui*, tending to remind you of incarceration in past lives. The solution is to tack up pictures of live objects to bring energy into the space. Alternatively, hang a dart board with your supervisor's picture on it.

Finally, you must remember that working in a cubicle is not unlike living in an apartment building -- you've got neighbours on every side. To ward off potential hostile relations with your associates, slow down the flow of *chi* with wind chimes or a loud radio. Don't be dissuaded by the scowls on your co-workers' faces -- they're just jealous of your good *feng shui*.

With minimal expense and a bit of muscle power, you should be able to reorder your workplace environment to obtain a perfect balance. Good cubicle *feng shui* can be yours. Just don't disturb it by bringing any work into your office.

"Bob Moore" The Toronto Star March 26, 1998

I recently tried to play a telephone prank on a co-worker by leaving her a phoney voice mail message from a "Bob Moore." The prank failed but for some reason Bob Moore lives on.

Once I had revealed my failed joke, I found it easy to continue to refer to "Bob" as if he really did exist. And my co-workers joined in. Despite Bob's physical absence, we enquired as to his health, his habits and his whereabouts.

At first, Bob Moore took on the role of my alter ego - a special imaginary friend who could bail me out of tight situations. But before long, Bob became my doppelganger - an evil twin who was constantly in hot water.

Co-workers would ask about Bob's whereabouts and I'd tell them that he was goofing off somewhere or getting into some kind of fun trouble. Pretty soon, it became easy to blame Bob for anything that went wrong in the office.

"Did you ever find that missing file?"
"Oh, Bob must have taken it."
"Why isn't that project completed yet?"
"Better ask Bob."

At the risk of sounding a bit deranged, I have to admit that Bob Moore seems to have become the conscious manifestation of my id. Or in more understandable terms - Bob's the bad dude I'm not allowed to be.

I can't play hooky from work but Bob can. I can't lose the file and pretend I never had it but Bob can. I can't make rude comments to young comely women but Bob can.

I've come to believe that everyone needs a Bob Moore - someone to take the blame or to play the joke or to pursue the fantasy. We should all develop our own personal alter ego, someone who can absolve us of all those faults, habits and cravings that might get us into trouble.

When my boss wants to know why my latest task isn't completed, I can just tell him that I passed it on to Bob Moore and I haven't heard back from him. And if that's not good enough for him, he can create his own alter ego (Frank Gold, say) to bail him out when his boss turns on the heat.

I'm sure others could also benefit from this new approach to human relations. Bill Clinton, for example, could have saved himself a whole lot of trouble if he had just been able to blame his own Bubba Smith for whatever skullduggery went on in the Oval Office. And Pope John Paul II's workplace might benefit from a Fred II, say, who could take the heat for any unpopular papal pronouncements.

My workplace is already a happier, healthier place thanks to Bob Moore. Whenever someone's accused of a mistake, Bob did it. Whenever we can't answer an enquiry, we refer the person to Bob. And whenever there's talk of downsizing, Bob Moore's name tops the list.

Now, we've had a lot of fun so far with Bob Moore. And my co-workers are even joining in with their own imaginary pals. But there may be a problem looming on the imaginary horizon.

Already I'm finding myself blaming Bob or referring to Bob a little too quickly. Sometimes I'm forgetting Bob's origins (or non-origins) and actually believing in his existence. Other times, I get worried that maybe Bob's plotting behind my back to get my job.

I'm sure this is just a passing phase and that things will get back to normal soon. If not, Bob Moore has one more thing to answer for. Bob? Bob? Can you hear me, Bob? Bob, this isn't funny anymore.....

"A Lesson in Bureaucracy"
The San Francisco Chronicle   June 8, 2001

      Welcome to the Bureaucrat Institute. Congratulations on choosing a career as an obfuscation and complication specialist. Start out learning the basics from paper shuffling to the telephone runaround. Then learn the skills you'll need to add red tape to any organization. Here are some useful courses:

-- CABLE, PHONE AND SEWER REPAIRS: This course will teach you how to maximize residential street disruption. Use sophisticated mathematical models and computer scheduling programs to optimize the number of times any given street must be dug up to repair just about anything. What appears to the average person as random inefficiency actually requires skillful planning among numerous private companies and public agencies.

-- BILLING: Complicated service bills don't just happen by accident. They're the products of decades of deliberate development. You'll learn the complex formulas that connect dates and hours to interest rate increases and climbing or sliding scales. In the municipal arena, see how mill rates are related to school taxes and water usage to sewer charges. When puzzled customers come looking for answers, you can give them more than they bargained for.

-- RECYCLING AND WASTE MANAGEMENT: Learn how to complicate a simple idea. Start with the concept of recycling garbage with one blue box for weekly collection. Add a black box for paper products and a green box for organic waste. Be adventuresome. Add different colors for different materials such as cardboard, Styrofoam and more. Learn the vagaries of collection scheduling, including random pickup day rotation and holiday weekend roulette.

-- PARKING SIGNS: Let your imagination soar! Start small with the production of the standard "Parking" or "No Parking" signs and work up to sophisticated creations such as multiple assigned sections in a single company lot or odd/even day, alternate side-street parking. Get even more creative and try an abstract collage of different, inconsistent parking signs on the same street pole.

-- FORMS, GLORIOUS FORMS: Paper is the lifeblood of any bureaucracy. While others adopt the computerized option, you'll learn how to stick tenaciously to the paper path. Learn the difference between an LDC-01 (pink) and an LDC-02 (blue). Find out how you can create your own form while carefully adhering to the minimum $25 fee and triplicate requirements.

If you finish all these courses, there is always our postgraduate program. We have courses in everything from Principles of Mazes to Dealing with Pesky Elected Officials. When you've completed our course load, you'll be well on your way to a satisfying career serving the public above and beyond their actual needs.

"Nice Work if You Can Get It"
Stitches Magazine   May, 2002

As the recession drags on, more and more people are being thrown out of work. In this high tech world, the assumption is that you need more training to get another job. But that's not necessarily true. There are lots of high paying jobs out there that need little or no training. Jobs like:

Economic forecaster

Here's a job that requires no expertise and no results. Of 54 private sector economists surveyed by *The Wall Street Journal* last July, only two predicted a recession in 2001. And as for accurately predicting future economic trends, most forecasters fail to come even remotely close. All you need to set up shop is a newsletter and a dartboard to help you decide if GNP growth will be 1, 2, 3 or 4%. It doesn't matter what number you pick since, even if you're wrong, no one will notice a year from now.

Political pundit

Do you have opinions? Do you like sharing them with others? If you answered "yes" to those two questions, you're ready for a career in political punditry. Worried about a lack of political knowledge or expertise? No problem. Just pick an issue, choose a side and start pontificating. If you need studies or statistics to back you up, there are institutes, think tanks and academics galore who will be happy to provide you with support for any view you might choose.

Editorial writer

See "Political pundit" above. This job has the added advantage of anonymity.

Lobbyist

Do you like arguing? Have you been accused of never seeing the other guy's side? If so, you may have a career in political lobbying. All it takes is a stubborn insistence on supporting only one side of a contentious issue and an ability to write cheques to political officeholders who agree with that opinion. Pick your favorite vice (tobacco, drugs or alcohol) and you can be its new advocate.

Financial advisor

Hang up a shingle and you've got a new career. Remember, it's not your money that you're playing with so don't worry. And as for client advice, any old random selection of stocks, bonds and funds will suffice so long as you give it a classy name like The Sterling Account or The Power Portfolio. Irate clients can be mollified with a standard industry cliché like "Now's the time to buy more", "It's just a temporary correction" or "Stay the course."

President

Are you a U.S.-born citizen? Are you 35 or older? If so, consider a job as America's chief executive. Recent officeholders have shown that little knowledge or expertise is required. As for experience, part time governance of a southern state will usually suffice. Although you will have to compete in an election, you don't necessarily need to get more votes than your opponent to win.

Prime Minister

Not a U.S. citizen? Not looking for too much responsibility? Then consider a job as Canada's leader. Like your American counterpart, you have to win an election but only in your local riding. Then once you've been chosen party leader, it's free sailing for as long as you want. (Position restricted to members of the Liberal Party.)

Member of the Senate

Remember the great times you had in college? Well, here's a chance to relive those days and get paid, too. Just like your old alma mater, you only have to attend occasionally. But unlike your old school, the Senate is not a four-year institution. So long as you're still breathing, you can kick back and party 'til you're 75. But apply soon because there are only 105 seats available and they fill up fast.

"A Death by E-mail Misadventure"
The Ottawa Citizen   April 12, 2000

  Excerpts from "The Collected E-mail Correspondence of David Martin" as submitted in evidence in District Court action No. T-43-98:

....

January 10, 1997
TO: John Barber
FROM: David Martin
Dear John,
  They gave me a computer at work and I have no idea how it works. Some young tech guy showed me e-mail so I'm sending you this message and hoping for the best. If you get it, please let me know even if you have to phone. God, I can't wait for early retirement.
All the best,
Dave

....

February 3, 1997
TO: Help Desk
FROM: David Martin
  I can't open my WordPerfect program. I move the mouse so the little arrow on the screen points right at the WordPerfect icon but nothing happens. Please advise.

....

February 4, 1997
TO: Help Desk
FROM: David Martin
  Thank you for coming down to show me about single clicks and double clicks. I appreciate the assistance. However, I did not appreciate the comments about techno-peasants and digilliterates.

....

June 6, 1997
TO: John Barber

FROM: Dave Martin
Dear John,
 I visited the World Wide Web today! What a rush! I feel like I have the world at my command. Unfortunately, I don't know how to search so I haven't actually accessed a web site yet. Still, I was there - on the Web.
Yours electronically,
Dave

....

August 16, 1997
TO: Martin Morris, VP Operations
FROM: David Martin, Senior Program Officer
 As requested, I have prepared the quarterly sales projections. You have asked me to send the file as an attachment to this message. Unfortunately, the file must be reformatted before I can transmit it. I will fax a "hard copy" today and hope to be able to send the attachment tomorrow.

....

August 17, 1997
TO: Help Desk   "URGENT"
FROM: David Martin
 How do you send an attachment????

....

October 5, 1997
TO: Modern Love Products; Alice Arkel
FROM: David Martin
 Please send me the inflatable Ginger doll (no. A33-1) and two tubes of all-purpose lubricant (no. L22-5). Charge it to my Visa card (5689 9246 9786 0432). I appreciate your guarantee of discreet service and unmarked packaging.

....

October 6, 1997
TO: Alice Arkel, Chief Librarian

FROM: Dave Martin, Senior Program Officer
    Please accept my apologies for yesterday's message. It was just one of those office jokes which I inadvertently copied you on. Please be assured it will never happen again.
....

November 2, 1997
TO: John Barber; ALL USERS
FROM: Dave Martin
    Look at these attachments! Wow! If you want to see more, go to www.babeswithbigbutts.com.
....

November 3, 1997
TO: Martin Morris, VP Operations
FROM: David Martin, Senior Program Officer
CC: Alice Arkel, Chief Librarian
    My apologies to you and Ms. Arkel. Someone has apparently accessed my e-mail account or is using my computer at night to order pornography over the Internet. Believe me, I am as disgusted as you to discover the existence of such web sites as Babes With Big Butts.
....

November 4, 1997
TO: Help Desk
FROM: David Martin
    What does ALL USERS mean?
....

November 28, 1997
TO: Martin Morris, VP Operations
FROM: David Martin, Senior Program Officer
    I strenuously object to the removal of my Internet privileges. I have always diligently followed company policy regarding computer usage and it is unfair to punish me for a handful of inadvertent mistakes. If my privileges are not immediately reinstated, I will take appropriate action.
....

January 4, 1998
TO: Bob Brewster, Senior Program Officer
FROM: David Martin, Junior Program Officer
   Congratulations on your promotion you snivelling weasel! Pursuant to your request for copies of previous quarterly sales projections, kiss my ass!

....

January 19, 1998
TO: Ace Employment Agency; ALL USERS
FROM: David Martin
   Further to our telephone discussion, I have attached a copy of my resume and a letter of recommendation from Martin Morris, VP Operations. As I indicated, I have outgrown my current job and look forward to a more challenging position. Please keep my application confidential as I am sure my departure would be very upsetting for many people at my company.

....

January 20, 1998
TO: Alice Arkel, Chief Librarian
FROM: David Martin, Junior Program Officer
   Thanks to you and that wimp Morris, this is my last day. Consider the attachments from Babes With Big Butts my goodbye present to you. File these in your Dewey Decimal system. See you in court!

....

January 20, 1998
TO: Burger Barn
FROM: David Martin
   I accept your offer of the position of Head Fry Cook. I assume computer experience is not required.

....

CHAPTER TWO

HOME REPAIR

"I've Got a Handle on This"
The Ottawa Citizen   December 31, 2004

I'm not a handyman and I've never claimed to be one. The electrical, mechanical and plumbing worlds that inhabit our house are as alien to me as a parallel universe.

But this home repair deficiency of mine is far from a point of pride. There is always a slight tinge of shame when I must call in someone else to change a light fixture or fix a leaking faucet.

So when one of life's simpler domestic repair jobs appears, I readily take it on in hopes of salvaging at least some small scrap of my masculine dignity. If there's a light bulb to be changed or a picture to be hung, I'm your guy.

Recently, I thought I could expand my limited home repair repertoire by replacing a broken clothes dryer door handle. The thirty-year old plastic piece finally gave up the ghost and broke off one Saturday morning when I gave it a yank to get at the clothes inside.

The old door handle had a part number embossed on the back and it appeared that a replacement would easily snap into the rectangular gap now left in the dryer door. After quickly examining the situation, I concluded that anyone could do this job - even me.

I called the parts outlet of the dryer manufacturer. They had one handle left in stock and they were a five-minute drive away. This was going to be easier than I thought.

The only minor annoyance was that the replacement handle made of fifty cents worth of plastic cost $23. Never mind, I thought, that's a small price to pay to demonstrate to my wife that I indeed was possessed of at least some handyman skills.

Ten minutes later, I was back home with replacement part in hand. With a smile on my face, I descended the basement stairs whistling happily to myself as I prepared to effect the one-minute repair.

I slipped the new handle out of its plastic sleeve, placed it in the rectangular opening and snapped it into place. At least I thought I snapped it into place. When I went to open the door, however, the new handle came flying out of the opening.

On closer inspection, I could see what the problem was. The tiny plastic flange along one side of the handle hadn't snapped under the metal frame of the dryer door.

No matter, I thought, the application of a bit of force will snap the handle into place. But a bit of force didn't suffice. Neither did a lot of force.

At first, I took care not to damage the handle. After all, if I inadvertently broke the tiny flange, our dryer door would be handleless and I'd be out $23.

But as my efforts became increasingly fruitless and the sweat began pouring off my forehead, I discarded rational thought and employed more and more primitive methods. First, I tried using a rubber mallet. Then I tried kicking it in. Finally, I attacked it with a screwdriver.

After an hour, I surrendered. The floor was littered with tools, my shirt was soaked in sweat and the "new" plastic handle was now chipped, gouged and not so new.

I returned to the parts outlet and asked for a refund. If I hadn't used my unorthodox installation methods, I might have had a chance. But once the parts guy saw the sad state of the handle, a refund was not in the cards.

He did, however, offer to order a warranty replacement handle free of charge. Given that I was the one who inflicted the damage, this was probably more than I could have expected. Given my luck with the first replacement handle, however, it was definitely less than I needed.

For now, we're doing just fine without a dryer door handle. In fact, the empty rectangular space works better than the plastic handle ever did. At least that's what I'm telling myself for now.

And what about the warranty replacement handle, you might ask? Well, when it arrives, I'll pick it up, bring it home and carefully place it on the shelf above the dryer. And there it will stay to await the inevitable day a real repairman comes to visit.

"Dude Where's My Rec Room?"
The Calgary Herald   September 25, 2004

Has the world gone renovation mad? If my wife and daughter are any indication, more and more people are getting hooked on decorating and makeover shows. From *Trading Spaces* to *Clean Sweep*, there's hardly enough room on the TV schedule anymore for an aging male to fit in the odd football game.

Now it wouldn't be so bad if the women in my house just watched these nefarious shows. But, of course, watching the shows inevitably leads to things like actual redecorating and renovating. And, without fail, I get caught up in the maelstrom of activity these new projects create.

I don't think there's much I can do to stem the tide of do-it-yourself mania. But assuming there are lots more males like me out there, television producers might want to consider creating new shows for this non-decorating demographic. Shows like:

While You Were Out

While the show's subject is out watching the game with his buddies, hidden cameras record what's going on at home. Which happens to be absolutely nothing. That's right. No crazy designers or wacky decorators giving his rec room an unneeded makeover. Just shot after shot of the big screen TV, moth-eaten couch and 40-year old beer fridge staying just where they are.

Trading Rec Rooms

Two guys get to trade rec rooms for a Sunday afternoon. See how each man adapts to a new environment and adjusts to his new surroundings. What may initially be off putting usually leads to the acquisition of a few new handy eye-opening hints. Hints like sewing a remote control pocket holder on the La-Z-Boy chair, putting your old TV on top of the new one for multiple-game viewing or simply using a portable beer fridge as a coffee table.

Just Sweep

Watch as a team of expert cleaners takes on the subject's messy home office. The team skilfully manages to clean the room from top to bottom without disturbing a thing. The unsuspecting owner comes home to find papers, books and files in the exact same disarray but with the room now suspiciously emitting a slight, pine-scented odor.

Why Not Wear It Again?

Rather than throw out the nominee's wardrobe and start over, the *Why Not Wear It Again?* team helps find a second life for all those outdated or worn out items. Find out how electrical tape can add months to the life of those favorite, hole-filled loafers. And check out how iron-on patches can extend the life of everything from shirts to pants to underwear.

It's A Fix

Your ceiling's falling, your deck's collapsed or your plumbing doesn't work at all. You could call in a new contractor to tear everything out and start over. Or you could learn to live with it. Check out how different men work around such problems using such simple, time-tested solutions as extension poles, cement blocks and portable toilet rentals. And, when all else fails, the ultimate solution: contact a real estate agent.

Weekend Worriers

Lots of men spend the weekend worrying that the tasks waiting for them in the job jar will interfere with what's really important, namely watching football on TV. *Weekend Worriers* puts those worries to rest with a wealth of shortcut solutions to everything from roof repair to plumbing fix-its. The show's "experts" demonstrate how quick-fix items like duct tape, Polyfilla and plastic sheeting can get the job done in plenty of time for the big game.

"Product Requires Assembly"
The Ottawa Citizen   September 7, 2004

Like most Canadians, I've shopped at IKEA. With clever furniture designs and reasonable prices, it's a bargain hunter's delight. And when you throw in those cute Swedish names for each and every item, it's downright irresistible.

But as with many bargains, there's a catch. And in the case of IKEA, the catch is that you have to assemble your purchase.

Now, in most cases, this turns out to be no big deal. Buy a table; cart it home in a box and in half an hour you've got yourself a sturdy piece of pine furniture.

Over the years, I've made my share of IKEA purchases. I started out easy with a SMEDVIK coffee table. Four legs, four bolts and a top. What could be easier? In a matter of minutes, I had a serviceable table that's still in use today.

Later, I graduated to a SMEDVIK kitchen table. No more difficult than the SMEDVIK coffee table assuming you remember to read the dimensions on the box and select the taller table. Unfortunately, I didn't. But apart from having to make an extra trip to the store to make a quick exchange, the assembly of the kitchen table was a piece of cake, too.

Last year, I ventured into more difficult territory with the purchase of a RÖBIN computer workstation. This was a project that required more than the attachment of four legs. As indicated in the IKEA catalogue: "This product requires assembly."

In my case, that meant assembling the item twice. Once with the sliders for the keyboard tray upside down and a second time right side up. Nevertheless, in well under three hours, I had put together a functional workstation with a minimum of cursing and physical injury.

This year, I took a quantum leap in my IKEA experience. My eight-year-old daughter Sarah needed a new bed and she and my wife Cheryl proudly brought home the VRÅDAL loft bed.

Cheryl started the assembly process in Sarah's bedroom. But before long, I was called in to assist in the project.

And what a project it was. This was no mere SMEDVIK coffee table and it made the RÖBIN workstation look like child's play.

The VRÅDAL was not a half hour project; it wasn't even a

three hour project. It was more like a two day nightmare.

There were 27 pieces of wood, two metal railings, dozens of bolts and screws, a bag of small wooden dowels and a whole bunch of plastic fasteners. And, of course, there were two Allen keys which, in theory, is all you need to assemble the bed.

IKEA kindly supplies a handy instruction sheet with step-by-step drawings of how to proceed. Unfortunately, they don't include any written instructions. Written instructions like "Mechanically challenged customers beware - DON'T assemble the frame until you have screwed the metal crosspiece holders in place." Or "The steps are numbered for a reason, dummy - follow them in order."

As most people will agree, IKEA's furniture designs are very clever. By using wooden dowels, threaded bolts with countersunk cylindrical nuts and strategically placed holes in the wooden structural pieces, they allow the customer to effect easy assembly using only two small Allen wrenches and a coin. Or, in my case, three screwdrivers, two pairs of pliers, a hammer and a flashlight to track down the missing parts that rolled dangerously close to the floor vent.

After several false starts, Cheryl and I managed to get the headboard and footboard assembled. And once we actually took the time to look at the instructions in detail, the second attempt at constructing the overall frame proved to be successful save for the occasional bruised foot caused by one of the countersunk nuts falling from its hole.

By the second day, we had completed the task. The crosspieces were secured in place with the collection of plastic fasteners and we topped off the VRÅDAL with the mattress from Sarah's old bed. It now only remained for Sarah to christen the new bed with her first night of sleep.

Alas, that first night of sleep was not to be. It turns out that Sarah is not comfortable in an elevated space. Even with a guardrail, she was too afraid to sleep in the loft bed......ever.

And that meant dismantling the VRÅDAL. Which we did. Given our newly acquired expertise in loft bed construction, the dismantling process proceeded much more quickly and efficiently than the assembly.

We traded the VRÅDAL in for something far simpler and easier to put together. Something auspiciously called the RÖBIN bed with bed shelf. And true to its name, it ranked no higher than its cousin, the RÖBIN workstation, in its assembling degree of difficulty.

Now despite my most recent experience, I'm still a big fan of IKEA. They've got a great selection of well-designed, economical furniture. And their generous return policy is not to be sneezed at. All I'm asking is that they provide a little more warning than "This product requires assembly."

What I'd like to see is an assembly-degree-of-difficulty rating to warn mechanically illiterate shoppers like me. Maybe they could even adapt their Swedish branding system a bit to let the customer know, for example, if a particular item requires the skills of a KLÜTZ, a MÖRON or a P.ENG. Then, at least, I'd know my limits.

"Must-have tools for the not-so-handyman"
The Gazette   July 26, 2004

    I love duct tape. When it comes to home repairs, duct tape is the universal solvent of the not-so-handyman world that I inhabit. From the lint catcher on the clothes dryer to the tail light on the car, this magical material can hold just about anything together.

    But for the truly inept, you need more than duct tape in order to survive in the quick-fix world of home repair. My "tool box" also includes:

Bricks

    I haven't got a clue how to build a chimney or an interlock driveway. But I do know that bricks have lots more uses than that. From a doorstop to a self-defense weapon, you can never go wrong by keeping a small supply of these handy blocks around. Combined with old boards, they make useful and uniquely stylish bookshelves and closet organizers. And for installing the Christmas tree, I like to jam half dozen of these babies into a plastic pail.

Popsicle® sticks

    When it comes to filling holes or sticking things together, you can't beat Popsicle sticks. When that door lock is starting to fall off or you can't keep that screw in the wall, just break off one or more pieces of Popsicle stick and jam them in there for a nice tight fit. Handy, too, for the application of small amounts of glue, paint or sealant.

Small stones

    When your young kids present you with their latest collection of small stones, resist the urge to throw them away. These items can be very handy for any number of home repair chores. Fill up that hole in the driveway or the foundation of the house. Combine them with Popsicle sticks for those extra tough wedging jobs.

Old hockey sticks

    Most people throw out old or broken hockey sticks. Big mistake. Over and above their utility as sliding door security barriers, old hockey sticks serve a multitude of uses. No need to throw out that thirty year old lawn mower. Just replace the broken metal handle with a duct tape-affixed hockey stick fragment and you'll be cutting grass for years to come.

Hammer

    If you're like me, tools confuse you. With all those gears,

levers and sockets, a non-handy guy could do serious injury to himself. But there's one tool you really can't do without: the hammer. Not only is it useful in affixing nails, it can also help to insert Popsicle sticks and small stones. The hammer is also the option of last resort. When all else fails, attack your home repair problem with a hammer. It may not solve the problem but it will always make you feel better.

<u>Cellulose filler</u>

You may know it by a brand name like Poly-filla. However you know it, you better buy some. Don't be intimidated by the instructions on the package; it's easy to use. And it's great for filling all those holes in your house. Handy hint: If you're buying this stuff in bulk, it may be time to think about bringing in an expert for some major repairs.

<u>Sandpaper</u>

Always keep a sheet or two of sandpaper handy. If you're a perfectionist, you can use it to smooth out the rough spots in your cellulose filler patching jobs. But for the rest of us, sandpaper can also be useful. From prolonging the life of your lawn mower spark plug to smoothing off the rough edges of broken Popsicle or hockey sticks, sandpaper is a versatile addition to any non-handyman's metaphorical tool belt.

<u>WD-40®</u>

Finally, no home should be without the ultimate not-so-handy guy tool: WD-40. When duct tape, Popsicle sticks or sandpaper won't do the job there's always WD-40. Just spray it liberally on the problem area and let it stand for ten or fifteen minutes. If that doesn't work, just use your hammer.

"Fences? Hard work makes good neighbors"
The Gazette   December 1, 2003

In his poem *Mending Wall*, Robert Frost playfully asks his neighbor why they need a stone wall when there are no cows to stray. The taciturn neighbor replies: "Good fences make good neighbors."

Although I might not always have agreed with that sentiment, recent experience has taught me otherwise. Good fences do, indeed, make good neighbors. And so do good trees, good roofs and good driveways.

When it comes to home maintenance, I am neither handy nor ambitious. My idea of spending a sunny spring day involves a book and a chair rather than a scraper and a paintbrush.

But over the last dozen plus years, I have come to realize that not all people share my philosophy of home repair. When something starts to wear, fray, peel or crumble, most people are inclined to grab a tool and get to work.

I always figured this was a personal choice and that my laissez-faire approach was as valued and respected as the can-do ethic evidenced by my neighbors. After all, I didn't try to convince them of the necessity of pursuing leisure and they didn't try to persuade me to change my hedonistic ways.

On occasion, our philosophies would clash. When one neighbor wanted to extend the side yard fence, I chafed at the idea of spending several days of what, to me, appeared to be pointless labor. But when he offered to do the work himself and split the bill, I happily went along.

Some time later, the opposite neighbor pointed out that the lower branches of the two large pine trees bordering our shared fence were impinging on his yard. Thus, I was obliged to trim the lower branches of the two trees.

So it was with some surprise that I found myself attacking the large pine tree in our front yard. The lower branches of our "maintenance free" tree had grown so big that they were brushing up against our car. Thus, even though no neighbor had asked, I tackled the job of trimming its lower branches, as well.

At my wife's urging, I began the dreaded task. Using my handy pruning shears, I lopped off a couple of dozen low hanging branches and hauled them onto the lawn. For the next three hours, I cut, trimmed and bundled the branches into manageable piles for the garbageman and raked and bagged the remaining mess for recycling.

Amidst all of my sweating, grunting and groaning, I was periodically interrupted by various neighbors. One of my immediate neighbors came over to encourage me in my task. He commented on the great improvement and urged me to trim even more of the offending branches. He even lent me his pruning saw to make the task easier.

Some time later, the neighbor from the other side dropped by to survey the job and praise my efforts. According to him, the removal of the lower branches had made a huge difference. He offered me a beer and cheered me on.

As the job progressed, other neighbors dropped by with nothing but kind words for my work. Suggestions were made; encouragements were offered. Apparently there was a huge pent up demand on my street for the trimming of this particular tree.

When the job was finally completed, I was exhausted. My face was covered with sweat, my clothes were covered with pine needles and my arms were covered with scratches. I had to admit that the tree looked better with its new clean lines and open bottom. But had it been worth it?

According to my wife, yes. And according to half a dozen neighbors, yes. And to the extent that it bought me a couple more years of peace and quiet, even I had to admit that it may have been worth the effort.

The problem is that the removal of the pine branches has highlighted the poor repair of our driveway. With more cracks than a discarded Easter egg, our piece of macadam is long overdue for re-paving. Not by my estimation, of course. But if those glances I'm getting from my neighbors are any indication, I've got some more work to do.

"Appliance Apocalypse Now"
Stitches Magazine   August, 2002

> *Today's hackers are trying to mess with your computer. Two or three years from now, those same cyberterrorists could be trying to damage your cell phone, your pager or even the appliances in your house. Technology analysts say any device connected to the Internet, particularly those with the ability to send and receive e-mail messages, is a potential host for a computer virus.*
>
> *- The Globe and Mail, August 1, 2001*

April 10, 2004

Arrive home to find answering machine flashing and washing machine gyrating wildly. Hit play button and listen to eery message from unknown voice threatening cyber home terrorism. Turn off washing machine, open lid and discover home hacker has activated bleach dispenser in rinse cycle for this morning's load of blue jeans and plaid shirts. Not a pretty sight.

April 13, 2004

Answering machine flashing. It's him again. Same creepy voice mumbles threat about VCR. Race to rec room and rewind tape. My attempt to record *Godfather IV* overridden by hacker's instructions to tape *Rocky VII*. This is war.

April 14, 2004

Book day off work to monitor home appliances. All seems to be going well until door bell rings and delivery boy appears with twelve bags of unwanted groceries and computer generated order form bearing my fridge's electronic authorization. Foiled again.

April 15, 2004

Return to work but monitor home appliances through my workplace computer. All seems well. Head home. Answering machine light not flashing. Maybe he's moved on. No such luck.

Check stove to find temperature reset at 600 °F and roast beef inside burned to a crisp. Baked potatoes unrecognizable. What kind of person would do such a thing?

April 18, 2004

Can't take much more of this. Electric toothbrush unexpectedly attacked me this morning. Quickly removed cord to prevent further damage to tooth enamel. Considered making toast and coffee but thought better of it. Both toaster and coffee maker acting strangely. Don't know who or what to trust anymore.

April 25, 2004

Afraid to go to work. Tried opening car door but assaulted with threatening recorded messages: "Be sure to buckle up and die", "Your gas tank is empty, sucker", "You're due for your one billion mile maintenance - ha! ha! ha!" Quickly went back inside house and found dishwasher spewing steam and water over kitchen floor. Fridge and stove yelling at one another in computer generated voices. Head to basement and disconnect kitchen electrical circuits.

May 5, 2004

Victory will be mine! All of the regular electrical lines have been disconnected. I have severed the phone line, cut the TV cable and buried all the modems. All the dry and canned food have been moved to the basement. Filled three garbage pails with water before destroying the water meter. Furnace was the last to go. When it started switching back and forth from cooling to heating, I knew it couldn't be trusted anymore. Tore off fan belt and destroyed the motor.

June 10, 2004

I have won! The appliances are all dead, the phones are silent and the lights are out. Two men arrived today and confirmed my victory. They congratulated me but insisted that I leave the house because, as they said, the appliances may have friends. I reluctantly agreed. With electrical appliances, you can just never be sure. I asked for safe haven and was kindly given a padded room with no phone or appliances. Safe at last.

"When bad cars happen to good people"
The Ottawa Citizen   July 16, 2002

For years, we've had marriage counsellors. Then came family counsellors. And now we even have grief counsellors, those peripatetic therapists who descend wherever mass tragedy strikes.

But what about those other times in our lives when relationships sour or things go bad? Are we just supposed to suffer through them alone or will new specialists evolve to help us? Specialists like:

The Auto Counsellor

You're emotionally attached to your car; it's like a member of the family. But it's eight years old and starting to break down regularly. You're in no position to make rational decisions about this friendship. That's why you need an auto counsellor.

The auto counsellor will help you restore a more realistic, practical relationship with your vehicle. She'll remind you that a car is a machine, not a person; that cars do eventually wear out and that there are plenty more out there with lower mileage and longer warranties. In short, she'll help you let go.

The Real Estate Counsellor

You established a close relationship with your real estate agent. You went everywhere together for weeks and he seemed to genuinely care about your needs.

Now that you've bought a house, he's nowhere to be found. That "dry" basement is flooding and the "new" roof has a leak but he no longer returns your calls.

The real estate counsellor will help you get over that whirlwind romance. He'll wean you off the sweet real estate talk. No more mention of gleaming hardwood floors, beautiful cathedral ceilings and walk-in closets. Instead, he'll bring you back to reality with some tough talk about home inspections, budgeting and double down mortgage payments.

The Stock Market Counsellor

You talked to your broker every day, sometimes several times a day. You laughed and joked together. It was almost like being in love.

But somewhere along the way, thinks went wrong. You felt uneasy about investing everything in *porkbellies.com* but he assured you it was a winner. Now your money's gone and so is he.

That's where the stock market counsellor comes in. She'll help you get over your addiction to stockbrokers and the thrill of the stock market roller coaster. She'll show you how to establish a secure, loving relationship with term deposits and municipal bonds. Sure, they may not be sexy but at least they're there when you need them.

The Electoral Counsellor

He promised the moon and the stars and you believed him. Worse yet, you voted for him.

What do you do when the elation of an electoral victory gives way to the sad realization of broken promises and compromised positions? You turn to an electoral counsellor.

He'll help you put your life back together after Joe Candidate has crushed your heart. Forget about political rallies and platforms. The electoral counsellor will give it to you straight: "Never trust a politician."

The Counsel Counsellor

They said "Get a lawyer", so you did. And for years, you had a heady relationship. He told you over and over again how much money he was going to get for you.

At first you were skeptical, but eventually you came to believe every word he said. But then the jury found for the defendant and you never saw him again. He wrote occasionally but only to tell you that he was seizing your car or putting a lien on your house.

The counsel counsellor will help you put the nasty breakup behind you. He'll get you laughing again at lawyer jokes and remind you of what you secretly knew all along: lawyers are scum.

The Death Counsellor

A grief counsellor is great for the living. But what about the dead? If you've just passed over to the other side, you've got a lot of questions and a lot of anxiety to deal with.

The death counsellor will help make the transition to the afterlife a lot smoother. She'll help you deal with the bewildering array of post-life choices. Do you opt for purgatory? Is reincarnation for you? How many angels can dance on the head of a pin? With her help, eternity doesn't have to be forever.

"My Autoerotic Affair"
Stitches Magazine   March, 2000

We met three years ago and it was love at first sight. She was small, dark and sleek and I could sense that special spark of attraction.

I sidled up and introduced myself. "Like to go for a drive?" I said. She didn't object and before I knew it we were an item.

Those first few days were heaven. We seemed to be made for each other. We went everywhere together; did everything together. We were inseparable.

But soon I sensed that something was wrong. Our first weekend trip started out great. But on the way back, she had a run in her hose and insisted that we spend the night at a service center just off Interstate 81.

When we got home the next day, I began to get suspicious. Sure, I knew she was no spring chicken and that she'd probably been around the block a few times. But I guess I overlooked all that in the blinding glow of romantic love.

So I started to do a little checking. It turns out she was a little older than she claimed. And when I asked around, I found out she liked to get lubricated a little more often than she should.

But it was early in the relationship and I was willing to overlook these minor flaws. After all, maybe she'd change. That, of course, was the misguided wish of a hopeless romantic.

She didn't change. Things just got worse. The first rush of new romance quickly gave way to fights, breakdowns and bitter recriminations.

At first, she wanted small gifts. So I bought her hoses, belts and filters. But that wasn't enough; she wanted more.

She started demanding expensive gifts like ball joints, struts and tires. The bills started adding up and when I tried to talk to her about it, she'd just breakdown and I'd have to buy her even more parts.

After a while, we couldn't take trips anymore. Every time we ventured more than fifty miles, she'd simply stop and refuse to return home. I had to pay to get someone else to drag her back.

This tumult went on for months. But I was still willing to work on the relationship. Every time there was a fight or a breakdown, I'd suggest counselling and we would go to my local garage and try to work things out.

But it was no use. She had more problems than I could ever deal with. Just when I thought we had gotten over the worst, she blew a gasket and sent me into total despair. I was sure our relationship was over.

I agonized for days. Something told me that I needed a more reliable partner. But I couldn't imagine how I'd make it to work every morning if she wasn't there. So I paid the bill and vowed to try again.

Things did improve after that. We had some good times together. We even went on a trip without ending up in some backwater garage.

But the signs were still there. I guess I just chose to ignore them. She started drinking oil again. A little bit at first and then before long she was downing an entire liter at a time.

All my friends told me I was crazy to continue. "Get out," they said. "She'll bankrupt you." But I didn't listen.

Until that fateful winter day when she went over the line. The red line, that is. This time she didn't just blow her gasket; she went right off the deep end. The mechanic said she had a crack in her block.

That was the end. I helped her get another engine but I made it clear that I didn't want to see her anymore. She tried to convince me that this was the last time, that it wouldn't happen again. Maybe she was right. But I didn't have the energy to try. So I drove her to the edge of town and said goodbye.

Maybe it wasn't just her; maybe it was me, too. Maybe she'll meet some other guy who has an eye for a black '91 Honda Civic sedan with 150,000 kilometers and things will be just fine. But somehow I doubt it.

Anyway, I've now settled down with a green, four-door Toyota Tercel. She's not flashy or sexy but she's reliable. And this time I'm taking it slow. We're starting out with a four- year lease and a three-year warranty and we'll see how things go from there.

Maybe ten years from now I'll be one of those guys who brags about his high mileage partner who doesn't cost him a cent. Hey - a guy can dream, can't he?

"Poof goes the lightbulb"
The Ottawa Citizen   September 23, 1999

Electricity and I don't mix. For some reason, when I turn my mind to electrical repairs, my mind turns to mush. So I was surprised to find myself tackling a problem with an overhead recessed light fixture in our basement rec room.

For years, there had been a loose connection with an occasional annoying flickering from the light bulb. But recently, the flickering turned to darkness and I began to attempt rudimentary repairs.

For the first few days, I periodically pushed the glass plate covering the recessed bulb hoping that this would restore the connection. Sometimes it did, much in the way that a random kick will occasionally fix a malfunctioning television set.

But after awhile, my taps on the plate failed to elicit a luminous response. So I bravely stepped into uncharted territory and actually removed the plate covering the bulb. I pushed the bulb up; I pushed the bulb down. I partially unscrewed the bulb and then screwed it in tighter. Sometimes the light came on and sometimes it didn't.

My past history with electricity should have dictated that I stop there and call in someone who might know what to do - someone, say, like an electrician. But faced with an electrical quandary, the logical synapses in my brain once again gave out.

If there's a loose connection, I reasoned, then it must be in the socket and all I need to do is put something in there to tighten things up. As my left brain struggled weakly to object, the right side boldly insisted that I put a small piece of foil next to the base of the bulb to secure a snugger connection with the socket.

Even my three-year-old daughter knows that she isn't supposed to put anything into a light socket. But something told me that this little piece of foil would do the trick.

So I screwed the foil-encapsulated bulb into the socket and was greeted by a loud "Poof!" and instant darkness throughout the basement. Something had obviously gone wrong.

I admitted defeat and groped my way up the basement stairs to the cordless phone and called an electrician. I explained what had happened and he gently reminded me that it was not a good idea to put anything in a light socket other than a light bulb.

After he had me confirm that the bulb went "poof", he directed me back to the basement to the circuit panel with flashlight and cordless phone in hand. After banging my head on the furnace and my knee on a stray bicycle, I located the panel.

The electrician asked me to push each breaker switch all the way to the off position and then back to the on position. I diligently moved each switch right and left until I was greeted with a loud static noise on the cordless phone.

Once I finally realized that I had disconnected the circuit for the phone base upstairs, I hung up the phone, reset the breaker and waited for the electrician to call back. He soon did and after he stopped laughing, he suggested that we wait until the next morning to continue our investigations. I readily agreed.

Having suffered enough humiliation for one week, I decided to get an early start for work the next day. Just to be safe, I exited the house at 6 A.M. and left my wife to deal with the electrician. And for the immediate future, I think I'll let her plug in the kettle, too.

"The time and skills required of a real man"
The Ottawa Citizen August 9, 1991

In the past few years, there have been a number of surveys on the sexual habits of couples and the sexual division of labor. And they usually show that women work 26 hours a day and men barely manage to hold down their day jobs.

As you've probably guessed, I'm a bit skeptical of these surveys. In fact, I've recently discovered that there was really only one poll taken and that various magazines and newspapers just altered the results plus or minus four percent to create their own results.

But even the one original survey is flawed. Not on the sex stuff, mind you. It was thrown in just to make men think the whole exercise was legitimate. If you're a male and you see results that say men initiate sex 99% of the time, you're going to nod your head knowingly and be lulled into accepting the rest of the results as gospel.

So I was not prepared for statistics that showed women effectively working two jobs a day. But that's OK, I thought, if someone wants to paint an heroic portrait of woman as saint and martyr. A small price to pay for avoiding the joy of childbirth.

But the survey writer went too far when she twisted the results to portray men as slugs. Quite simply, I was incensed. This was another instance of statistics being used for evil rather than good.

For example, the survey found that many men tended to spend much of the evening watching TV. The implication, of course, is that, by doing so, men are avoiding their share of household labor. Unfair!

Men are not watching baseball, football and *Jeopardy* for selfish reasons. They're simply trying to acquire interests and knowledge to pass on to their children. They are courageously accepting the role of our society's cultural repository. It's a tiring job and this undoubtedly explains why most men feel the need to perform it in a prone position on the sofa.

And the survey also casts aspersions on what men do when they go to the workshop or the den. The underlying suggestion is that we've hidden a couple of beers and a copy of *Sports Illustrated* at these locations for our amusement. Not true!

In the division of labor poll, I don't think anyone took into consideration the extensive time and skill needed to carry out various projects in the workshop. Remember, a bird house is just a smaller version of a real house. So it shouldn't be surprising that it takes a few months of construction time.

And the den? Well, that's where we spend countless hours organizing the financial records. Conservatively, I'd say it takes at least 100 hours a year just to get the records in shape to be passed on in a shoe box to an accountant for some minor fine tuning.

And that survey is further flawed by restricting the division of labor to the house. There's a lot of work being done outside the back door that the surveyor just didn't count.

For example, women think that just because a man has racing stripes and a beer bottle holder on his sitdown mower that he enjoys mowing the lawn. Or that he likes wearing an apron with "World's Greatest Chef" on it as he burns various meat products on the gas barbecue (with optional beer bottle holder). No - these tasks are difficult domestic chores.

And no one seems to have considered the hazards involved in traditional male chores. Sure, it doesn't take long to haul out the garbage. But considering the toxicity of modern refuse, would you want the task? And what of the heroic legions who risk heart failure to clear driveways and sidewalks of snow each winter? And give thanks that you don't have to face the humongous child-eating spiders that lurk in the back of the garage.

Finally, there's childcare. Sure, men don't participate as much. But it's not our fault that we're genetically different. We didn't ask to be born with a diaper gag reflex. Otherwise, we'd be glad to help.

So let's put these survey results in context. I don't doubt that women are being stretched to the limit with their multiple roles. But don't forget - just because a man's lying down with his eyes closed doesn't mean he's not working.

CHAPTER THREE

PARENTING

"A toddler's handbook for parentcare"
The Globe and Mail   November 20, 1997

You're almost two years old and you're fast losing patience with those two adults who call themselves "mama" and "dada." If you hear the words "stop it" or "no, no, no" one more time, you're going to go mad.

Welcome to the "trying two's." As cute and entertaining as your parents can be, you must never forget that their ultimate aim is to manipulate and control your behavior. This is the stage where you have to put your tiny foot down and exert some discipline. If you don't do it now, there's little hope that you'll be able to train them properly in the years ahead.

The best place to start is with meals. I'm sure you've all experienced the frustration of trying to make your simplest food or beverage request known to your parents. It's surprising that so-called adults who can dress and feed themselves can't understand their own child.

But there are several surefire ways to get your message across. One method is to repeatedly point and shout until your parents guess which food or beverage you want. Another method is to overturn your soup bowl and milk glass until they finally clue in that you want something with sugar in it. If your parents start to become unreasonable, you might want to take drastic measures and fling your food around the room. This usually gets them back on track trying to meet your needs.

Another area which requires a lot of work is the bedtime ritual. For some reason, parents feel it's necessary to put you to bed at the same (early) hour every night. There's really no logic to their obsession and it can be very annoying. But they must be broken of this habit now.

There are different approaches you can take to this problem. You can refuse to physically move from the playroom although it's difficult to win a physical battle with mom and dad no matter how slow-witted they may be.

The better bet is to humor them through the early stages of the bedtime routine. But when push comes to shove and they try to put you in the crib, be firm and let them know clearly that you won't tolerate such treatment. This may involve loud pleas and complaints over an extended period of time. Chances are at least one parent will finally get the message and release you from the crib.

But if all your best efforts seem to fail and mom and dad stubbornly ignore your rational cries, it may be best to give up for the moment and go to sleep. However, to avoid giving your parents the impression that they have "won", it's best to wake up sometime in the middle of the night and get them up too. After a couple of sleepless nights, they'll be more amenable to your bedtime requests.

Similar approaches can be taken with other aspects of daily life. For example, if you don't want to take a bath, you can make it pretty difficult for mom and dad. But this is one area where you may not want to be too rigid. Sometimes it's healthy to let parents have a small "victory" so they can feel that they are asserting their independence. And really, who minds having someone else bathe them? If it makes them feel good, it's not much of a sacrifice on your part.

The keys to parent rearing are vigilance and consistency. No matter how tired you are or how trivial the task, you must be alert to your parents' attempts to control you.

Take the toy pickup, for example - an essentially meaningless exercise since the toys will only be brought out again tomorrow. The best way to handle this problem is to get a parent to help you. Put a token block or two away and smile cutely while the parent cleans up the rest.

Other areas require greater vigilance. Parents, as I'm sure you have noticed, will watch any garbage that's on TV. It's your duty to steer them away from the violence and pap that is all too common on the tube and direct them to more educational and calming shows like *Barney* and *Mister Roger's Neighborhood*. If they persist in their negative behavior, you may want to consider hiding the remote in the toilet.

The task ahead is difficult and there will be lots of times when you want to give up. But you must persist now before bad habits become too ingrained. Sometimes the job seems too hard, especially when you've got two of them ganging up on you. But remember, they're only parents and, with a little love and discipline, they'll do what you want.

"A toddler's guide to toilet training"
The Toronto Star   July 8, 1998

You're two and a half years old and life is good. You eat what you want when you want. You sleep when and where you like. Grown adults bathe and dress you. And, best of all, you can soil your diaper and someone else will clean up the mess.

It's been a struggle but it's worth it. You've finally trained those two folks called Mom and Dad to cater to your every need. Despite their initial resistance, they now know that your wish is their command and they've pretty much given up that annoying habit of trying to regulate your behavior.

But the price of freedom and leisure living is eternal vigilance. Your parents may seem compliant but you must always be alert to some new irrational request they manage to dream up.

Their latest demand is something they call toilet training. It has nothing to do with teaching tricks to the commode and everything to do with threatening your cushy lifestyle.

For years now (2½ to be precise), you've enjoyed the God-given right to urinate and defecate when and where you feel like it. And you've taken for granted the fact that Mom or Dad will change your diaper when necessary.

Now they've got the misguided notion that "pooping" and "peeing" (as they so cutely call your excretory functions) are to be restricted to certain times and places. In short, your two loving parents have turned into potty Nazis.

As with most of your parents' silly schemes, the best approach is to humor them. If they insist that you sit on that ridiculous toddler toilet seat, just do it. You don't even have to perform. Initially, at least, they'll be thrilled if you just sit there.

But after awhile, Mom and Dad are going to start insisting on some action. In particular, they want to see you pee.

The best way to handle the situation is to occasionally accede to their request. It's no big effort on your part and it's worth it just to watch the paroxysms of joy your parents will experience.

It's strange that grown adults can get so excited about a little urine but, for whatever reason, they do. The key, however, is not to "go on the toilet" every time. This heightens the drama and excitement for Mom and Dad.

Once you experience your parents' reaction, you may find it so entertaining that you use the toilet regularly just to see their faces contort and hear them shout "Good girl!" or "I'm so proud of you!" Big mistake.

If you show any consistency at all in your toilet habits, Mom and Dad are going to expect more of the same. Sad as it may be, you must break them now.

So if you've been using the toilet consistently for a few days, it's time to start peeing elsewhere. Beds, rugs, car seats - they're all fine spots. You'll find that it won't be long before your parents give up and start putting you in diapers again.

But remember, sooner or later, they're going to try toilet training again. So you may want to consider initiating the process yourself from time to time just to keep them off balance.

And if you do, you should take advantage of the situation. Mom and Dad are so anally fixated that they're willing to give you just about anything to see a little toilet action. Everything from candy to fancy underwear can be yours just for the asking.

Now after awhile, you may even want to use the toilet. Let's face it; no one likes to sit in a dirty diaper for too long. But when you do decide to kick the diaper habit, do it on your own terms and don't let your parents know. Because if they think their pathetic training attempts had anything to do with your change in behavior, the next thing you know they'll be trying to put you to bed before nine.

"A toddler's guide to summer vacation"
The Toronto Star   August 3, 1998

I just turned three and I have to admit, life is pretty good. I do what I want and my every wish is my parents' command.

But this cushy lifestyle didn't just happen; it took a lot of work. For as long as I can remember, my Mom and Dad have been trying to control my behavior. And for just as long, I've had to set them straight.

For some unknown reason, parents insist on trying to manipulate toddlers. But as cute and entertaining as parents can be, you can't let them get their way. If you give in now, you're just encouraging more of the same.

For three long years, I've been vigilant in thwarting my parents' irrational attempts at behavior modification. When they tried to put me to bed at eight o'clock every night, I resisted. When they insisted that I pick up my toys, I said no. And when they engaged in that barbaric practice known as "toilet training", I put my tiny foot down.

But all of that pales in comparison to something Mom and Dad call "summer vacation." To you, summer means playing in the park and fun in the sandbox. For your parents, however, summer means packing up the car, driving hours in the scorching heat and spending days or even weeks in some godforsaken frontier location.

You don't have much choice but to go along with this silly notion. But there are a number of things you can do to insure that Mom and Dad never make such a stupid decision again.

First, make your parents' trip to the vacation destination a living hell by crying, yelling and pounding your tiny fists. And when they stop for lunch, make sure you spill everything in sight and refuse to eat.

Even if you're tempted, do not nap. Mom and Dad are counting on that afternoon break. If they don't get it, they'll be weaker in the evening.

If your parents try to stop for some "fun" activity like hiking, be sure to slow things down. At the very least, insist that one of them carry you. A fun hike with a thirty pound toddler on one arm soon turns into Chairman Mao's thousand-mile march.

Once you've reached your vacation destination, that's when

the fun begins. Your parents think that the hard part is over and that their relaxing holiday is about to begin. Their guard is now down and this is the time to strike.

By dinner time, you should have them so worn out that they'll accede to any of your requests. If you want milk in a bottle, it's yours. If you want Fruit Loops with ice cream on top, it's yours. If you want ice cream in a bottle, no problem.

In fact, you'll find it's kind of fun to make up crazy requests, watch Mom and Dad scramble to fulfill them and then change your mind. When they bring you chocolate ice cream, cry and ask for strawberry. When they bring you strawberry, ask them what happened to the chocolate.

Without a nap, you're going to be tired but not as tired as your parents. Persevere, break through the wall and stay up as late as you can. While you're jumping up and down on the hotel bed at 11 P.M., Mom and Dad will be walking around like zombies muttering to themselves.

Chances are that after two or three days of this, your parents will come to their senses and realize that it's time to go home. Once you know that the car is homeward bound, ease up on your folks. After all, once again, you are victorious.

But if you sense there's still some residual resistance, you may want to drive home the point about the inanity of summer vacations one last time. As your car rolls into the driveway at the end of the trip, throw up in your car seat. That should end any talk of summer getaways for a long time.

"Whose birthday is it, anyway?"
The Ottawa Citizen   October 25, 1999

I just turned three and life is good. I eat what I want, I sleep when I want and I do pretty much as I please.

This cushy lifestyle didn't just happen; it took a lot of work. After three long years of effort, I've been able to train my parents to do just want I want.

So I was a bit surprised by their latest attempt to assert some control over my life. It's something they call a "birthday party" and you need to be aware of what happens when Mom and Dad undertake this new project.

Without my input or permission, my parents organized a celebration of my third birthday. They invited three of my friends which was fine with me. But they also invited the parents. Let's face it; who needs more parents?

Mom and Dad spent weeks hyping this thing which should have clued me in to what was ahead. Given their level of excitement, I knew this bash could never meet their expectations. If only they had consulted me first.

Mom spent days sewing an elaborate fabric donkey with a pin-on tail. Apparently this was to be part of some organized game for me and my friends. The fact that we had little use
for it almost reduced Mom to tears. But she only had herself to blame. A little toddler consultation could have avoided this parental heartbreak.

Dad, too, had his hand at organizing a party activity. He dreamed up something called musical chairs only to lose his temper when we decided to run in all directions rather than in an orderly circle around the chairs. If he'd only asked, I could have warned him against any organized activity.

It was only when I took over and gave some direction to the party that things took off. We didn't want organized activities; what we were looking for was something disorganized. So, with my lead, we started playing a random game of hide-and-seek. Now that was fun!

But my parents, of course, put a quick end to that activity and insisted that I start opening my presents. Initially, I thought this was a great idea until I started unwrapping the gifts from Mom and Dad.

I don't know if they're senile or just stupid but after opening the first package, it became abundantly clear to me that they had not gotten me the one item I had been requesting for weeks - Flip and Dive Barbie.

I overheard Mom telling Dad that she decided against Flip and Dive Barbie because it wasn't politically correct. I let them know in no uncertain terms that it would have been easier all around to just get me what I wanted. After my little tantrum, I think my parents learned a valuable lesson in the politics of toddlerhood - if I say I want it, then it's correct.

Once the gift fiasco was over, Mom and Dad finally did something right - they brought out the birthday cake. But they embarrassed me in front of my friends by only providing vanilla ice cream. Why didn't they just bring out bread and water!?

After cake and ice cream, Mom and Dad pretty much lost control of the party. Fights erupted over cake, over presents and over games. And when it was time to go, my friends were understandably resistant. Two hours had passed and we'd only had about ten minutes of fun.

I hope my parents learned their lesson. This birthday party was for me, not for them. I think they got the message and will be willing to shell out a few bucks next year. Then my friends and I can go to Wally's Party World where they really know how to have fun.

"The cruel kindness of Mistress Sarah"
The National Post   February 21, 2000

Four years ago, as a 45-year-old first time father, I thought that I was prepared for the arrival of my new daughter Sarah Jean. After all, my wife and I had attended every pre-natal class, read every baby book and bought every contraption from a crib mobile to a breast pump. In fact, I felt so prepared that I was even convinced that I could do pinch hit breast feeding duty if called on.

But I wasn't prepared for Mistress Sarah, that tiny voiceless dominatrix who skilfully forced me into a new world of sadomasochism that I never knew existed. With no more than a look or a tiny scream, she made me run the emotional gamut from tears to joy. One minute she would be giving me a wide-eyed heart-touching look and in a flash she was screaming for my obedient subservience.

The most devious part of Mistress Sarah's cruel kindness was her refusal to identify the next task I had to perform in order to stop her from torturing me with cries and screams. I knew she was crying but she wouldn't tell me why. Hence I found myself performing a whole range of degrading tasks she dreamed up in the hopes of hitting on the one she wanted performed NOW!

In my naiveté, I first tried to meet her demands with a loving hold and a gentle voice. Mistress Sarah pretended to be satisfied with this pathetic attempt but quickly punctuated the air with another cry that let me know I had failed.

Hoping it might have been a demand for food, I quickly passed Sarah to my wife who temporarily placated her with a breast feeding. We were both prisoners to Sarah's twin pleasure domes. My wife was bound and attached to those breasts that were no longer hers and I was reduced to passing food and drink to my wife in the hopes that sustenance would keep the breast milk flowing.

But Mistress Sarah only took temporary delight from the breast. Without warning, she would unlatch and then turn her head to me with a look that said the fun is over. That's right - it was time to enter the dungeon of doom with the mysteriously named "changing table" equipped with tiny instruments of torture.

I broke into a sweat knowing that I had to perform the diaper change. And I had to perform it perfectly if I was to be spared "the scream." If I missed one step or misplaced one item, I had failed and

I would be punished. And even if I succeeded, my only reward was a tiny diaper destined for the garbage.

After a day of catering to our tiny daughter's demands, my wife and I prayed for some nighttime relief. Alas, it was not to be for Mistress Sarah, in her wisdom, had decreed that day was night and night was day. Rather than incur the wrath of Sarah, we accepted her cosmology and packed in what "daytime" sleep we could when Sarah was peacefully snoozing away. But we lived in fear that she might next have decided to reorder the days of the week or even the alignment of the planets.

Every second day, my wife and I tried to exact some small measure of revenge on the six pound dominatrix masking as our daughter. When she least expected it, we grabbed her and subjected her to a bath, an activity which she clearly detested. But before we could revel in our little victory, Mistress Sarah brought us to our knees with a powerful wail and a new undecipherable demand.

This cycle of servitude went on every day with Sarah dictating and my wife and I complying. Sometimes Sarah bestowed small favors like a brief chance for a shower or a ten minute meal. But the leash was short and she quickly whipped us back into shape.

I adjusted to my new S & M lifestyle and I even eventually learned to decipher the wordless commands of my mistress. And believe it or not, I loved every minute of it. I only wish that they had made an orthodontic pacifier for dads.

"Parenting quiz stumps this dad"
The Ottawa Citizen   August 30, 2000

An Ontario educational TV network that shall remain nameless recently sent me a booklet entitled "Are You the Parent You Want to Be?" The booklet consisted of a four-part "self-assessment quiz" to test your parenting skills followed by seven pages of advice for those who might need it.

Confident in my status as a superdad, I eagerly took the quiz secure in the knowledge that I would have no use or need for the final section. The quiz had four categories of questions designed to assess "relationships", "routines", "learning" and "community." Each question asked me to rate how often I engaged in a particular behavior or activity with my child from "never" to "always."

As I took the quiz, I took on a rather smug, self-satisfied air since it appeared to me that I was racking up huge points as I checked off the "usually" box for most questions. I became quite self-congratulatory while noting that I usually praised my five year old daughter Sarah, that I usually encouraged her and that I usually fell asleep before she did.

Once I answered all the questions, I assigned the appropriate points and added up my score. On a page entitled "How did you do?", I was asked to measure myself against other parents. To my disappointment, my not insubstantial point total placed me squarely in the third of five categories. The accompanying text essentially said that as a parent I was just okay. I was invited to review my answers and work at improving my parenting skills.

The instant guilt that this test summoned up led me, of course, to read the advice section and vow to improve. Quite apart from Sarah's welfare, this was serious business. Based on the scoring scale, I wasn't even in the top third in the superparent competition.

I was crushed. All that effort and all that love and I was nothing more than an average father.

But then I saw the devious plan behind the quiz. The sponsoring television network was looking for donations and nobody coughs up like a guilty parent.

Sure enough, when I checked the other scoring categories, the quiz creators had pulled a fast one. With a possible total of 180 points, the first category was for those scoring less than 20 and the fifth for those above 170.

The scoring legend gently chided the former group when, in fact, it should have been alerting the police to possible child abuse or the presence of a dead parent. To score less than 20, you would have had to have been raising your child from another planet.

Similarly, the quiz extravagantly praised the high scoring group who clearly either didn't know how to take tests or were congenital liars. Mother Nature herself would be hard pressed to score over 170 on this test.

Once I realized that there were really only three legitimate categories and I was "almost" in the "real" top one, my guilt started to subside. But not enough to avoid the network's ploy.

Despite running the emotional gamut from guilt to anger, taking the quiz did highlight one important fact. That nameless TV network from Ontario had been supplying my daughter with first class, commercial-free programming for the last four years and it was time for me to show some support.

So I cursed the marketing wizards and sent the network a donation. With that, I figured I deserved an extra ten points which put me in the real top category where I knew I belonged all along.

"Apocalypse this week: diary of a parent survivor" The Christian Science Monitor January 17, 2001

SUNDAY:
0800 hrs. Mommy just left on a six-day camping retreat leaving me to guard the troops which consists of my four and half year old daughter Sarah. With almost five years of hand to hand parenting training under my belt, this assignment should be routine.
1100 hrs. Supply of video training films featuring various Disney characters has been exhausted. Boredom rears its ugly head.
1300 hrs. In order to avoid terminal tedium, I order the troops on an aquatic exercise at the local YMCA. Operation "Family Swim" deemed a partial success.
1600 hrs. On our return trip to the barracks, we stop at the video store to stock up on more current Disney training films. Wisely opt for week-long rentals.
2100 hrs. Lights out for Sarah.
2200 hrs. Lights out for Dad.

MONDAY:
0900 hrs. Advance planning and reconnaissance has paid off. Sarah deposited in Camp Playcare at the Y while Dad engages in much needed aerobic exercise. Buys time to plan afternoon maneuvers.
1300 hrs. Military stroke of genius! Double troop numbers with Sarah's friend Mikayla and head for afternoon movie matinee. Who says single parenting is hard?
1500 hrs. Declare partial surrender. Two trips to canteen and one to washroom have depleted supplies and patience. Minor injuries incurred as Sarah is scared by the movie and Mikayla gets her legs caught in the seat. Quick retreat to home to await troop pickup by Mikayla's parents.
2100 hrs. After successful meal of hot dogs and viewing of new Disney training film, lights out for Sarah.
2130 hrs. Lights out for Dad.

TUESDAY:
0900 hrs. Spring surprise on troops with unconventional morning

bath followed by expedition for more rations at local supermarket. Eventually succumb to Sarah's repeated requests for fruit rollups.

1300 hrs.   Mild panic sets in until I remember Mommy had signed Sarah up for an afternoon field camp in arts and crafts. Unfortunately, camp is ten miles away and lasts only two hours. I wander the halls aimlessly until it's time to go.

1600 hrs.   Another military stroke of genius! I invite Sarah's friend Bridget over for dinner. While they practice maneuvers with Barbie dolls and accessories, I prepare elaborate macaroni and cheese dinner complete with chopped up dill pickles as requested.

2100 hrs.   After driving Bridget home, it's lights out for Sarah.

2115 hrs.   Lights out for Dad.

WEDNESDAY:

0900 hrs.   Mikayla's mom wins medal of honor for taking Sarah for the morning. Dad retreats to the Y for aerobic exercise and more strategic planning.

1300 hrs.   Much anticipated two-hour arts and crafts break fails as Sarah insists Dad stay for entire session. On the plus side, Dad reacquaints himself with the lost art of papier-maché.

1600 hrs.   Thanks to rigorous pace, Sarah and Dad both take a much needed nap. I feel I have regained the upper hand.

2100 hrs.   Advantage lost as downside of afternoon nap becomes painfully apparent.

2300 hrs.   Dad and Sarah finally fall asleep together on Sarah's bed.

THURSDAY:

1000 hrs.   Partial surrender declared as emergency excursion undertaken to Toys-R-Us outpost. After half hour of negotiations, parties settle on shiny dress up skirt for $5.99. Dad skillfully avoids $19.99 Barbie purchase.

1300 hrs.   Toys-R-Us purchase buys two hours of privacy during afternoon arts and crafts camp. Dad revels in rare chance to read grownup book.

1730 hrs.   Grandparents invite troops to dinner but allow Dad to retreat and enjoy dinner alone at home.

2100 hrs.   After picking up Sarah from grandparents, we head home and it's lights out for Sarah.

2105 hrs.   Lights out for Dad.

FRIDAY:
0900 hrs.   Once again take advantage of Camp Playcare for Sarah at the Y and engage in strenuous exercise. It is only a matter of hours now until Mommy's return.

1300 hrs.   Arts and crafts camp finally fulfills earlier promise as Dad spends entire session reading newspaper and dreaming of tomorrow's R&R.

1805 hrs.   Mommy calls to inform troops that she will be later than expected as both Sarah and Dad fight back tears.

2200 hrs.   Mommy arrives to find Sarah asleep and Dad muttering line from *Apocalypse Now* ("Oh the horror!"). Sarah awakes and gives Mom heartfelt greeting. Dad joins in group hug and gladly relinquishes command.

"Whatever you do, parents, do not follow this advice" The Ottawa Citizen July 3, 2000

Attention parents! Tired of the endless battle for supremacy with your kids? Had it with the constant fights over food, clothes and bedtime?

If you've reached your limit in the child rearing wars, it's time to change your strategy. Get rid of all those parenting guides written by self-appointed experts whose kids left home years ago. They're just designed to make you feel guilty.

Instead, give yourself a break and follow "Dave Martin's Guilt-free Guide to Parenting." Follow these seven easy rules and you'll never feel inadequate as a parent again. In fact, you're probably following most of them already.

1. Let them eat cake!

Ease up on those dietary restrictions. Why try to stuff broccoli and spinach down your kid's throat when you can barely tolerate the stuff yourself? Instead, go with pizza, hot dogs and ice cream. They're all fine foods high in nutrients and preservatives.

If you still feel it's necessary to aim for a balanced diet, that's OK, too. But just loosen up a bit. For example, if you want your kids to eat some vegetables, don't forget about French fries and ketchup, the latter having received the endorsement of none other than Ronald Reagan.

2. Bedtime is anytime

Forget about those early evening fights over bedtime. Stop driving yourself and your kids nuts with unrealistic expectations about when they'll go to sleep.

Remember, bedtime is anytime. Let your kids decide. They can't outlast you so just wait until they drop and then drag them off to bed hassle free.

3. Television is your friend

Should you permit half an hour of TV viewing a day? Is one hour too much? Forget about those silly limits. If you ever hope to read the newspaper in peace, you've got to remember that television is your friend.

Kids love TV. They'll watch it all day if you let them. So why not let them? If nothing else, it's good training for adulthood.

4. Kids are meant to be dirty

Bath time fights can be loud and wet. So why bother? Kids get dirty and they stay dirty. Give them a bath and two hours later they're dirty again.

Here's an easy rule of thumb. If your child doesn't smell, don't bother with a bath. Before you know it, that nightly ritual will be down to once a week. And think of the water you'll save!

5. Toys are not meant to be picked up

Everyone tells you that your child will learn responsibility and self-discipline if he's required to put his toys away each night. Nonsense. All he'll learn is that he can drive you nuts by resisting and delaying.

And what difference does it make anyway? Those same toys you help him put away tonight will be hauled out first thing tomorrow. Why not just leave them where they are? If you find things getting a bit messy, just sweep them into a pile.

6. Kids wear the darnedest things

You've spent a small fortune on little Susie's wardrobe but she won't wear that pretty pink dress she insisted you buy her last week. Instead, she wants to wear her striped orange t-shirt with the yellow plaid pants.

You know what? Let her. It will save you all that hassle fighting over clothes and you won't even have to dress her. If you need to dress up something fancy, buy a doll.

7. Tantrums are embarrassing

Every child rearing expert has an opinion on what to do when your kid has one of those public meltdowns in the grocery store. One says you should talk to the child, another says you should hug him and still another tells you to remove the child to a quiet spot.

Well, forget about it. When little Johnny is lying on the floor, pounding his fists and screaming at the top of his lungs, all you'd like to do is vanish. So, why not? Just walk away and pretend he's not yours. Chances are he'll follow along shortly. If he doesn't, you can always return to pick him up when store security calls you.

So throw out that parenting manual and start living again. Master these seven easy rules and stop worrying. Remember, if *laissez faire* can work for economists, it can work for parents, too.

"Duelling over diapers"
The Ottawa Citizen   April 24, 2004

Through my eight years of child rearing, I've noticed a trend in modern fathering: the macho dad. For generations, fathers had limited involvement in their children's lives, particularly young children. Dad worked, brought home the pay cheque and was not expected to be an active childcare participant.

However, with the advent of women's liberation and the increasing number of two-income couples, the modern male was required to assume more parental responsibilities. And over time, dads expected and even wanted to be more involved in the raising of their children.

Cultural observers have noted the changes this new paradigm has wrought. Men are now getting in touch with their sensitive side and achieving deeper and earlier emotional bonds with their children.

All this, of course, has been to the good. Greater parental involvement by fathers can only help in the healthy emotional and physical development of today's children.

But despite this dramatic cultural shift, some things don't change. Whether it's excess testosterone or some primitive hunter instinct, we men can't seem to get involved in anything unless it's competitive. And if there isn't an element of competition, we'll invent one. That's why the modern dad has been transformed into the macho dad.

When my daughter Sarah was an infant, I remarked to a male friend that it often took me several minutes to change a dirty diaper. He scoffed at my pathetic efforts and claimed that he never took more than a minute to do the dirty deed.

Another male friend belittled my minimal participation in Sarah's bath time routine. According to him, if I was a real man, I should be bathing my daughter nightly by myself.

I was even chided for my limited involvement in feeding my infant daughter. Lending the occasional hand to spoon some baby food down Sarah's throat was clearly not good enough. Ironically, I even began to feel guilty and less manly because I couldn't breastfeed her.

More and more, I found that I was being judged by other dads. Could I stop Sarah from crying? Could I feed her? Could I burp her?

Could I bathe her? If not, maybe I wasn't a real man.

And this new duel of the dads didn't end with infancy. Once Sarah became a toddler, I was faced with the playground competition. You don't just take your kid to the park anymore. Now you compete with the other dads in everything from swinging to running to sandcastle building. Sit on the park bench, like I often did, and you're a loser.

As my daughter got older, the pressure was on to teach her new skills. If I was a true modern dad, I was expected to be out there with Sarah teaching her to swim, to ride a bike and to balance a chequebook. Never mind that I was over fifty and had an aging back. If I wanted to earn my fathering merit badge, I had to be a hands-on dad.

Then there's the long-term care competition. When Sarah was 21 months old, I took her on a 1500 mile plane ride for a three-day visit with friends. I thought I was top dad until I met two other fathers on the same flight who promptly informed me about their younger children and longer trips. My paternal ego was quickly deflated. The fact that there was no extra seat for Sarah on the flight home didn't help. Battling with a cranky toddler on my lap for a three-hour plane ride did little for my superdad self-esteem.

It's not like I was incompetent. I could carry out all the basic functions from diaper changing to bathing to feeding. And if my wife had to be away for a few days, I somehow managed to do it all by myself. But that was no longer enough.

When I talked about caring for Sarah solo for extended periods, women were impressed. But not men. If I did three days, the other dads had done four days. If I did a week, they had done two weeks. No warm, fuzzy sharing of common feelings and experiences for us guys. This was war.

Sarah's eight years old now and I face the coming years with trepidation. Who knows what a modern dad is expected to do these days? At the very least, I anticipate assuming new duties like assistant soccer coach, dance class driver and math tutor. Beyond that, I shudder to think what will be expected of me. Cycling partner? Computer guru? Marathon trainer? It's enough to reduce a father to tears - if tears were allowed.

Don't get me wrong. I think it's great that men are becoming superdads. But maybe it's time to also recognize the darker side of the modern father. Let's get this macho parenting out into the open and hold annual Modern Dad Olympics. Then we can really settle who's the best diaper changer, the best feeder, the best burper or whatever. And I can finally get back to taking afternoon naps guilt-free.

CHAPTER FOUR

FINANCES

"Just Zig When I Zag"
The New York Times   December 8, 2000

Congratulations on subscribing to The Martin Report, the financial newsletter that has savvy investors talking. You'll now be privy to the latest happenings in the life of Dave Martin, the investment barometer, and thereby be able to predict upcoming financial trends with unrivalled precision.

Here's how it works. Fifteen years ago, we discovered an uncanny new prognostication tool: the financial decisions of Dave Martin. Dave Martin doesn't predict future trends in the marketplace. He inadvertently signals the end of current ones.

Back in 1990, Mr. Martin bought a house. Subscribers to our newsletter were immediately informed since that purchase signalled - correctly, as events soon proved - that the hot real estate market of the late 1980s was about to peak. Property owners who read our newsletter sold at maximum returns, and purchasers held off for a year or two to effect huge savings.

Market watchers benefited again in 1995, when disappointed with the returns on his meager stock portfolio, Mr. Martin switched from United States companies to Japanese equities. The Martin Report issued a special bulletin urging investors to sell their Japanese stocks and go back to Wall Street. Needless to say, those who did fared well.

In 2000, Mr. Martin purchased three new suits. Our readers were immediately notified, as that transaction signalled the end of formal dressing in the workplace and the beginning of the new casual look at the office. Savvy subscribers bought heavily into khakis and polo shirts.

If you had been a subscriber last year, you would have been among the first to hear that Dave Martin had finally decided to forego the compact car market and instead purchase a gas guzzling land yacht. That heralded an imminent rise in gas prices. Those in the know were able to buy heavily into oil and gas stocks.

This month's bombshell is the news that Dave Martin just signed on for high-speed Internet service. Market watchers have long wondered when the PC revolution would end. Now we know it's just about over.

So, unload those wired stocks and start investing in the

wireless revolution. You can look forward to solid growth, at least until such time as Mr. Martin contemplates the purchase of a router or a cell phone.

Considering his current psychological and financial state, we don't look for major purchases by Dave Martin any time soon. We also see no indications of future vacation travel. Thus, we remain bullish in the consumer sector.

The coming months may be a bit of a bumpy ride for many investors. But if you keep tracking the economy with the advantage of The Martin Report, there's no reason you can't realize double digit returns for years to come.

"Have you really made it?"
The Chicago Tribune   July 17, 2001

It used to be easy to acquire status. All you needed was a big house and a big car. But now lots of people have big houses and big cars. So what do you do to these days to show that you've made it? Check out these new visible status symbols in ascending order of importance:

1. Owning a sports-utility vehicle.

    Owning two SUVs.

    Owning a Toyota Echo to drive to your multicar garage to pick up your SUV.

2. Washing your face with spring water.

    Washing your clothes in Evian water.

    Washing your SUV with Perrier water.

3. Taking a cab to work.

    Driving to work.

    Saying "fill `er up" at the gas station.

4. Traveling to New York City.

    Living in New York City.

    Leaving New York City.

5. Eating organic.

    Eating fusion.

    Not eating.

6. Only having basic cable.

    No cable.

    No TV.

7. Having a dog.

    Having a kid.

    Having six kids

8. No computer.

    No answering machine.

No phone.
9. Planning a garden.

   Having a garden.

   Having a gardener.
10. Sending your kids to private school.

    Having a reserved parking space at your kids' school.

    Sending your kids to public school to learn the hard way.

    Finally, there's the ultimate in status. To show you've really made it in both a minimalist and ostentatious way, carry no keys, no money and no ID. The less you have to carry, the more important you are. Unless, of course, you get hit by a bus.

"The Dialectic of Garage Sales"
The Ottawa Citizen   May 28, 2005

Karl Marx was right. Capitalism sucks - big time. And I have the empirical data to prove it.

Two years ago our family participated in that springtime ritual of free enterprise - the garage sale. To be more precise, my wife organized and conducted the sale and my seven-year old daughter Sarah and I went along for the ride.

For days beforehand, my wife had made preparations for this grand event. She culled through countless items from our daughter's brief past including the small collection of infant toys that Sarah was grudgingly willing to part with. With ads placed and signs prepared, we were ready to go.

After a less than restful sleep, we arose early Saturday morning to set up tables and haul out our unwanted goods. Bleary-eyed and sleep deprived, we had to face the cheery smiles of "morning person" bargain hunters who insisted on doing business before we were ready to open. With a few grunts and groans, I made it evident that they might want to come back later if they were serious about making a purchase.

Fuelled by coffee and doughnuts, we were eventually up and running. Cars stopped, people looked and some even bought. We went through the mandatory haggling process as in "Will you take one dollar?"; "No, it's two dollars"; "OK, I'll take a dollar and a half." It seemed that the cheaper the item, the tougher the bargaining.

As the hours passed and the sun rose in the sky, I began to wonder if this free market venture was worth it. Although a number of low price items were disappearing, none of Sarah's pricier baby appliances had left the lot. I was beginning to feel despair.

Finally, business picked up. We unloaded Sarah's car seat. Someone took the infant wading pool. The turtle sandbox found a new home. But by the end, we were still stuck with far too much stuff that had to be dragged back into the basement.

Exhausted and discouraged, we shut down the sale at 2 P.M. For some reason, post meridian sales are limited and post-2 P.M. transactions are non-existent. At that point, I didn't care; I was just glad it was finally all over.

Now I'm not saying the day-long event was not without its

pleasures. After an unusually cold and damp spring, it was nice to be outdoors on a sunny May day with near-normal temperatures. And it was also nice to see our neighbors after the long winter hibernation.

But if a garage sale is supposed to illustrate the joys and efficiencies of capitalism, ours showed me instead why I'm still a socialist at heart. The two aims of such an exercise are to clear out the garage (or, in our case, the basement crawl space) and to make money. On both counts, we failed miserably.

After eight hours of a steady (albeit light) stream of potential customers, we had not made a significant dent in our storehouse of expendable goods. Lots of small items were quick to sell and a number of Sarah's toys found new owners. But the large, space-taking items like strollers, baby seats and high chairs remained unsold only to be returned to their apparent permanently assigned locations in our basement.

A quick accounting of our work revealed an even bigger shortcoming. Gross proceeds from the sale rang in at $52. Pretty pathetic revenue for a full day, not including all the preparation time.

But that doesn't tell the whole story. As in any capitalist enterprise, there were also expenses. Ten dollars for materials to make signs, five dollars for coffee and doughnuts and twelve dollars for the classified ad. Net proceeds: $25. Once we had factored out the eight dollars that went to Sarah for toy sales, that left $17.

Now some might say: "Hey, what's your complaint? Capitalism works. You made a $17 profit."

That's true. But I think it was actually a better example of the crushing exploitation of the masses. Considering that my wife and I both put in an eight-hour day on Saturday and she spent an equal amount of time preparing for the sale, I figure we ended up making about 70 cents an hour. Slave wages by any measure. Plus I still can't safely navigate our crawl space.

So I've decided that when it comes to garage sales, I'm a socialist. Better to just give your excess goods away than to spend a tortured day for peanuts. As a wise old prophet once opined: "No one ever said on their deathbed that they wished that they'd held just one more garage sale."

At least when it comes to garage sales, I'm with Karl Marx. So maybe next spring, instead of having another one, we'll just have a great big May Day giveaway. It'll be shorter, easier and way less painful. And I can go golfing instead.

"Tax, where is thy sting?"
The National Post   April 26, 2004

Two words explain why women live longer than men: income tax. Although feminism has tended to even out the domestic workload between the sexes, there still remain three holdovers from the patriarchal days of yore. One is "taking out the garbage." Another is "mowing the lawn." And the third is "doing the taxes."

Now no man has gone to an early grave from a surfeit of garbage hauling or lawn mowing. But many a male has seen years taken off his life by that annual rite called filing your tax return.

It begins in early February when those first investment records show up in the mail. They signal the beginning of the dreaded season known as tax time.

You try to put it out of your mind but every week there's another reminder: a charitable receipt, a tuition record or an RRSP contribution. And when you finally receive your T4s in early March, your blood pressure's already higher than last summer's golf scores.

As spring arrives, the days inexorably tick away towards that dreaded April 30th deadline. Although you have weeks to plan your attack, it never seems like enough.

The tax department's package that arrived in the mail weeks ago still sits unopened on your desk, mocking you for avoiding its contents. Should you open it now and do a preliminary review? Doesn't it make sense to check out the contents and see if you need to order that extra form to claim "non-capital losses on foreign investment dividend income carry forwards?" Wouldn't it be a good idea to review your records and see if you have an official receipt for your "charitable" donation to the Fraternal Order of Froth Blowers or the sales slip for that new Gameboy you "needed" for your home office?

But that's the approach you tried last year and we all remember what happened last year. It was a disaster. As was the year before and the year before that.

So maybe this year you'll try the "defer and avoid" method. On the theory that financial matters tend to be self-resolving over time, you've decided to wait until the final weekend of April to do your taxes.

But however you approach the task, there are two things you

can count on: total frustration and never ending stress. Even when you think you're almost done, the tax department throws you a curve.

You might even be on the last page, mere lines away from claiming that huge refund you've been counting on. And there it is right below line 432: "If you are claiming the non-fungible mortgage interest repayment credit for your former primary residence, you need to submit form UR-SCRWD-9." Form UR-SCRWD-9 is, of course, in the process of being revised and currently unavailable.

The ways in which you can be thwarted are infinite. For every calculation or plan of attack you formulate, the tax department will devise five different moves to block you. Not that you really need their assistance in what inevitably becomes a self-defeating exercise.

How can you defeat your own best efforts? Let me count the ways:

1. You fill out and mail in your tax forms early only to receive another income or investment slip in the mail the next day.
2. You wait until the end of April but after you finish, your bank sends you a "corrected" T3 with their sincere apologies.
3. You spend all day completing the forms only to discover that your addition mistake on page one has been carried through to every subsequent calculation in the form.
4. You challenge the income tax gods and decide to forego a working copy and fill out the forms in ink thereby necessitating the use of an entire container of White Out.
5. You decide to work on your taxes on a Sunday afternoon unaware that the tax department's 1-800 information line closes at 1 P.M. on weekends.
6. You forget to buy batteries for your calculator and are left to rely on your grade four mathematical abilities.
7. You succumb to the tax department's siren calls to take the easy route and file on-line which results in an unplanned trip to the computer store to have them retrieve all your data from some inaccessible sector on your hard drive.

Doing one's taxes is not a three or four or even a five hour job. It is a three-month marathon. Beginning in early February and ending in late April, it consumes many of a man's waking hours and more than a few of his nightmares. It literally takes years off our lives.

Now women are probably thinking to themselves: 'What a

bunch of wimps. This is just some simple income tax form. It's not like they have to give birth or anything.'

Maybe not. But most women only go through the birthing process two or three times. Men have to face the taxes every year. No wonder we die first.

As Benjamin Franklin once wrote: "In this world, nothing is certain but death and taxes." And, as I'm sure Ben would agree, after years of doing one, the other doesn't look so bad.

"Fund, fund, fund"
Stitches Magazine July, 1999

I recently attended a presentation for participants in a managed investment plan. A managed investment plan is a sophisticated investment vehicle that allows you to have experts manage your life savings for a fee in order to achieve a rate of return roughly equal to the alcoholic content of light beer. I won't identify the company involved except to say it was a trust company with the word "royal" in its name.

The presentation was held in a large room in a nondescript recreational facility. Two men spoke. One spent about fifteen minutes telling us how our investment plans worked. The other fellow spent half an hour giving us economic forecasts based on complicated computer models, detailed statistical research and the alignment of the stars.

As I listened to the two presenters, I looked around and saw a sea of grey hair and bald heads. At age 48, I realized that I was probably the youngest member of the audience. Maybe I'm in the wrong plan, I thought. But then it dawned on me; you had to have a minimum investment to be in this managed plan and that's why there was a disproportionate number of senior citizens.

The fact that we had at least some money to invest is why the company was giving us this presentation. As a bonus, we even got a little wine and cheese after the talks. This was our reward for using the company's services. My primary goal for the evening was to consume enough wine and cheese to cover the annual fees I'd already paid.

This all got me to thinking. If my little nest egg entitles me to a wine and cheese party in a recreational facility, what do the rich folk get?

Say you're in the $250,000+ range of investment holdings. I doubt that you'd just get cheese and crackers. I imagine those folks are probably invited to a nice dinner in a posh setting and that the presentations are made over coffee and dessert. I bet the wine is different, too - probably imported rather than domestic. And I even suspect that this crowd gets different expert forecasts and predictions than we did.

What about the $500,000+ investor? I'm betting he doesn't

even have to leave his house. Some guy probably comes to the door with a video presentation, a case of wine and a wheel of cheese.

The one million dollar investors are undoubtedly in a league of their own. I'm sure these guys get wine, cheese and dinner, too. But I wouldn't be surprised if they're flown somewhere like Barbados to enjoy it. And I'm guessing the economic forecasts they're receiving are a lot rosier than ours.

And what about the really rich - those folks who have millions? Well, they probably don't get anything. And why not, you might ask? Because these are the guys who've been managing all those investment plans for the last five years. They haven't got time for dinners or wine and cheese presentations. They're too busy laughing all the way to the bank.

"How I became a believer in consumer society"
The Toronto Star   June 3, 1998

Some years ago I received a consumer product survey in the mail. That's one of those multi-page questionnaires designed to find out if you eat, sleep and bathe and, if so, which company's products you choose to perform those functions with.

My first reaction was to chuck the thing out. But after some thought, I rescued the envelope from the garbage. Completing marketing surveys was, after all, part of my duty as a member of our free enterprise system.

The letter accompanying the survey confirmed the importance of my participation. A "research manager" named "Carole Smith" stressed the need for my assistance. According to Ms. Smith, the jobs of farmers, truckers and manufacturers hung in the balance. And companies who "truly care about their products" just wanted a brief peek at my life to help "make their products truly better."

I wasn't quite sure how my answers would ameliorate the state of our marketplace, but I instinctively trusted Carole Smith. More importantly, her letter also informed me that if I sent in a completed survey I would be eligible for "some fabulous prizes." And even if I didn't win "some fabulous prizes", I would be receiving discount coupons to help me purchase all those products I would be helping to improve.

The kicker was Ms. Smith's invitation to "have fun!" in completing the survey. 'Sure - why not?' I thought. What with my car dying and the washing machine going on the blink, I hadn't had my quota of fun for that week.

Now some people's idea of fun would have been to fill out the survey in the most illogical, senseless pattern imaginable. For example, checking off nothing but canned spaghetti sauce and mayonnaise. Or leaving the section for soaps, cleaners and deodorants blank thereby creating a rather odious consumer profile.

But my conscience dictated otherwise. As a member of a free market society, I was under an obligation to help our corporate citizens. My "fun" would be in knowing that I was helping to stem the onslaught of generic products by keeping our brand names safe and secure.

So I slowly slogged through the survey form, marking a little "x" in the appropriate boxes. Now I can't say that it was "fun" to complete the survey. But it sure was an eye opener. In fact, upon completing all the questions about brand name products, I was surprised that I had lived past thirty. According to the survey, my diet was barely sufficient to sustain human life. It seemed to consist primarily of soft drinks, frozen juices and something called "adult cereals" (Sleazios immediately came to mind).

There were huge yawning gaps in my diet. No seasoned rice, no lemon pie filling and no granola and fruit snacks. No chili sauce, no tomato juice and no canned and dry soup mix. My dietary deficiencies had me reaching for a brand name multi-vitamin.

There were equally large chasms in my lifestyle. No dog food (ergo - no dog), no cat food (ditto) and no tampons (no mate). No diapers, no furniture polishes and no automatic dishwasher detergent. The only good news was that I didn't yet need bladder control products.

The final depressing blow came during the completion of the "general information" section. Income, employment status and dwelling type all seemed okay. But then there was the series of questions asking if I owned (1) a compact disc player, (2) a gas barbecue, (3) a home computer, (4) a microwave oven or (5) a video recorder. I couldn't put a single "x" in that section.

This was no longer "fun" - I was severely depressed. My diet was a disaster, my social status was questionable and my lifestyle was clearly deficient. Fun? I was crushed and I wished that I'd never seen Ms. Smith's survey.

I thought that I would be helping my country. Instead I became a pitiful wreck desperately looking to buy anything from VCR's to furniture polish just to avoid survey embarrassment. I turned into the consumer from hell in a pathetic attempt to effect some serious lifestyle renovations.

Thanks to Ms. Smith's devious survey, I am now a husband and a father living in a suburban bungalow with two cars in the driveway. And I own everything from a CD player to a food processor and there appears to be no end in sight.

So please heed my warning. When you receive one of those consumer surveys in the mail, go with your first instinct - toss it out. Sure, they seem like fun - but they're dangerous. You may think you're happy and have all you need but Carole Smith knows otherwise. So just head for the garbage pail and remember that old Latin maxim - 'caveat surveyor.'

CHAPTER FIVE

RELATIONSHIPS

"Breakfast and a movie"
The Ottawa Citizen   April 23, 2005

Breakfast and a movie. How in the world did it come to this?

It seems that every other issue of every women's magazine on the planet has an article about saving your marriage. And the number one piece of advice in these articles is to make time for you as a couple. But if you have young children, you know as well as I do that "couple time" is pretty much an imaginary concept.

Life wasn't always like this, of course. Back in our childless days, my wife and I would frequently go out. One of our favorite activities was dinner and a movie.

Then baby arrives and things change. No one's got the energy to go out at night. If baby is sleeping, that's a good time for both of you to also catch a few zzzs.

But thanks to all those magazine articles, we worried about our relationship. If there was no "us time", surely our marriage was at risk.

So we occasionally summoned up the courage to have a night out. We'd call up a babysitter and take a stab at that old standby, dinner and a movie.

Big mistake. If we weren't nodding off during dinner, we definitely had a hard time staying awake through the movie. And even if we did manage to remain conscious, the only topic of conversation during our precious couple time was our infant daughter Sarah who was at home doing exactly what we should have been doing: sleeping.

We soon realized that dinner and a movie was no longer for us. All it meant was the outlay of extra money for a babysitter, the loss of a good night's sleep and a disrupted routine.

But we didn't want to give up on this concept of couple time. After all, lots of magazine writers (probably single and childless) were urging us on and we didn't want to disappoint them.

So we came up with a new approach: something we called movie and a dinner. We hired a babysitter for the afternoon and early evening and headed out to a matinee performance followed by the early bird special at a local eatery. This option worked surprisingly well.

Not only did we get to spend time together when we were both conscious and reasonably coherent. We also never had a problem getting a babysitter. After all, we were usually home by 7 P.M., long before the sitter's own social life commenced.

But once our daughter passed the toddler stage, the movie and a dinner option didn't work so well. Sarah had weekend activities and obligations. Or she wanted to have a friend over. Or she just wanted to spend more time with mommy and daddy.

As a consequence, we forgot about movie and a dinner. We were too busy occupied with family time and kids' activities. Once again, couple time became the lowest priority.

But we hadn't forgotten our magazine writer friends (probably sadistic and divorced). So we searched for a new option. Now that Sarah was in school and life was more normal, we thought maybe the old dinner and a movie approach would work. It turns out it didn't.

Although life had returned to something approaching normalcy, it turns out that we had gotten older in the process. The thought of staying up past ten o'clock no longer had any appeal.

But surely there had to be some way to find time to spend together. According to our writer friends (probably rich with two nannies), our marriage depended on it. There had to be something we could do on a regular basis. Something that would allow us that precious "us time" without costing a fortune or disrupting our sleep.

Finally, this year we hit on the ultimate couple time solution: breakfast and a movie. With Sarah in school, every so often we take a weekday to ourselves. And what do we do? You guessed it.

We go out for a nice leisurely breakfast where we can listen, communicate and, best of all from my perspective, eat. And then it's off to the local cinema multiplex which just so happens to start showing movies at ten or eleven in the morning.

We pick out a first run feature we'd like to see, put up our feet and enjoy two hours of uninterrupted movie viewing. Sometimes we even get the entire theater to ourselves.

After the movie is over, we have a whole array of options. We can go out for lunch, go to a coffee shop or browse in a bookstore. We can do a bit of shopping, watch another movie or, my personal favorite, go home and have a nap.

I think this is an option with legs. So long as Sarah is in school, we can continue to do breakfast and a movie. The only potential problem I see is that everyone reading this piece is going to start doing the same thing and the breakfast restaurants will be crowded and the morning shows at the cinemas will be sold out. Oh well, if that happens, there's always takeout breakfast and a rental movie.

"Beware the Stepford Husband"
The Ottawa Citizen   February 2, 2005

As I approach my 55th birthday, I sense a transformation. I'm not talking about the wisdom that allegedly comes with age. Nor am I talking about falling hair, jowls and chest although they're definitely in the cards.

Rather, I'm speaking of a change more attitudinal than physiological. Subtle signs suggest that my manhood is at risk. In short, I fear I am becoming a Stepford husband.

I'm sure you've noticed them, the aging males with the vacant stares and the eager-to-please smiles. They can often be seen accompanying their wives on lengthy shopping expeditions in the grocery store or at the mall. They are the ones pushing the cart or holding the bags without complaint.

These poor souls willingly spend hours in a variety of female haunts from beauty parlours to kitchen stores to dress shops. The lucky few at least get to sit in the waiting areas provided. Fewer still find a magazine to read.

I often wondered what happened to these once proud men. Had some strange plague of obsequiousness infected them? Or had they simply been neutered by the passage of time?

As I reluctantly stare seniorhood in its wrinkled face, I search for answers. Is it the inexorable physical decline that causes these men to change or is it their waning libidos? Whatever the cause, it seems to gradually sap the male essence from their beings.

It appears to start slowly with a subtle shift in the inter-spousal relationship. Where once these men argued with their wives, now they find themselves simply agreeing. "Are you crazy?" has, over time, given way to "Yes, dear" as the preferred response to any spousal request.

Gone are the boys' nights out. Gone, too, are the manly activities of old. No more weekend-warrior-wannabe attempts at playing softball, hockey or squash. No more post-game gatherings to talk about sports, cars and women. And no more misguided attempts at handyman pursuits. All these things seem to be now left to younger, more virile males.

The other signs are there, too. No longer do these aging men wear their once-treasured, patch-covered pants and hole-filled t-shirts. Somewhere along the way, they lost their spirit of resistance and started to let their wives dress them.

Like some senescent Ken dolls, they are "properly" decked out in "acceptable" clothing. Most have willingly adopted the common wardrobe of the Stepford husband: a buttoned-down, Oxford-cloth shirt, "relaxed fit" stretchable Dockers and a pair of sensible shoes.

In short, they have been domesticated. Like some jungle cat tamed for the circus, the Stepford husband now docilely performs the household chores. Gone are the remonstrations of old. Now he unquestioningly cooks, cleans and washes as if it were his single goal in life. His youthful motto "Let's party" has been replaced by "I live to launder."

Is this some mid-life, andropausal adjustment? Can all these changes be explained by hormonal ebbs and flows? Is that why these aging souls now listen to their wives and engage in actual conversation? Does that account for why they have a strange new urge to "share their feelings?" Can this be the reason they sometimes find themselves switching from the football game to watch a bit of *Oprah*?

This switching from football to *Oprah* is yet another sign of the Stepfordization of aging men. Their years of constant channel surfing and complete dominion over the TV remote have ended. Not only can they cede control to their wives, they can now miraculously sit there silently and watch as she switches from one home improvement show to another.

From time to time, the Stepford husband's former ego will briefly reassert itself and he will revert to old patterns. You might find him watching a quarter or two of football, wearing his old sweat pants or even leaving the toilet seat up. But a quiet yet firm word from his wife quickly brings him back to his new reality.

Some might think this altered state would be unpleasant. They assume that a Stepford existence must be demeaning and emasculating. Superficially, that might be true. But, according to these transformed males, once you surrender to your spousal siren, life becomes simpler and happier.

After all, what could be more satisfying than relinquishing control to your spouse? No more decisions to be made about what to wear or what to watch on TV. No more pointless arguments over household chores and daily routines. All that is replaced by the comforting knowledge that someone else will now decide.

As the years pass and the shopping trips become more frequent and my pants creep up closer to my armpits, I'm told I will find a new peace of mind. Apparently it is futile to resist. Like it or not, I, too, am destined to become a Stepford husband.

"29 ways to know he's not cheating"
The Ottawa Citizen   April 3, 2004

     Dear Abby recently reprinted her list of 29 signs that your husband may be cheating. From "buying new underwear" to "wanting to try new love techniques", these 29 clues supposedly help nail a philandering spouse.
     I'm troubled by lists like these. Why do we have to accentuate the negative and assume men are cheating? Why not publish a list of 29 signs that your husband may be faithful? A list like this:

1. Buys himself new sweatpants.
2. Regularly replaces batteries in the TV remote.
3. Scratches himself in all the usual places.
4. Hides the chips and dip.
5. Grunts hello in the morning.
6. Leaves the toilet seat up.
7. Refuses to answer the phone.
8. Shaves his face but not his back.
9. Thinks cologne is a city in Germany.
10. Likes to pat his belly.
11. Raises hypothetical questions such as, "Do you think it's possible to watch more than one football game at a time?"
12. Spends an inordinate amount of time at the hardware store.
13. Never washes his hockey equipment.
14. Leaves his underwear on the bedroom floor.
15. Has no clue where the laundry soap is.
16. Thinks a depilatory is a conservative pharmacist.
17. Gets excited when you talk about sit-down mowers.
18. Seldom matches a pair of socks.
19. Gets a $10 haircut.
20. Forgets to trim his nose hairs.
21. Wants sex every Saturday night.
22. Wears pajamas to bed.
23. Thinks grooming is a city in China.
24. Buys beer by the case.
25. Won't leave the house on the weekend.
26. Shows a sudden interest in navel lint.
27. Plays minesweeper on the computer.

28. Leaves the house in the morning smelling of dirty socks and returns in the evening smelling even worse.

29. And the telltale sign of a faithful spouse? Sometimes you wish he weren't, just so you'd have a better dressed husband.

"Romancing the stoned"
Stitches Magazine   March, 1998

One of the biggest threats to average folks today is the relationship expert - the pop psychologist or TV therapist who keeps telling you that your emotional life is a failure. Books, talk shows, infomercials, videotapes, audiotapes, weekend seminars - wherever you turn there's some busybody trying to change you. Who needs it?

Well, forget about it. The last thing you need to do is take valuable time away from lounging and TV watching to "revitalize your relationship" or "improve your sex life." All of that involves work and work, if you'll remember, is the one thing we want to avoid.

Now I know you're going to find it hard to resist the siren songs of the relationship gurus. Especially when your spouse or significant other is whining in your ear about your failure to cook dinner or mow the lawn or remember some anniversary. But resist you must.

If you're having doubts about your ability to persevere, I've devised a little quiz to reassure you that you're average and normal and don't need an emotional makeover. Just answer the following ten questions, follow the scoring directions at the end and see where you fit in.

1. When your partner says he/she feels lonely and unappreciated, you say:
    a) "I love you sweetheart" and give him/her a hug.
    b) Nothing and hope he/she will go away.
    c) "Why don't you get a dog?"

2. You've been married ten years and your spouse suggests that your marriage has become routine and stale. You....
    a) Say that you're willing to do what it takes to rekindle the spark.
    b) Nod knowingly and change the channel on the TV.
    c) Suggest a threesome with the new blond neighbor.

3. Your spouse suggests a romantic getaway weekend to resuscitate your flagging sex life. You....
    a) Agree and offer to make the reservations.
    b) Grunt and say "whatever."
    c) Inform him/her that it's out of the question because of the upcoming Superbowl/Jane Eyre film festival.

4.   Your spouse is due home from a business trip in two hours. You....
   a)   Clean the house and prepare a nice dinner.
   b)   Move all the empty beer bottles to the basement.
   c)   Leave a note stating that you'll be back after midnight.
5.   The baby wakes up crying at 2 A.M. You....
   a)   Quietly get up and change and feed the baby.
   b)   Nudge your spouse and inform him/her that the baby needs attention.
   c)   Move to the downstairs bedroom to get some sleep.
6.   Your spouse announces that your in-laws are coming for a one-week visit. You....
   a)   Help clean and prepare the guestroom for their visit.
   b)   Order extra booze to help you through the week.
   c)   Book a one-week getaway to Las Vegas.
7.   You open the refrigerator and notice that the milk carton is empty. You....
   a)   Run down to the store and buy a quart.
   b)   Leave a note reminding your spouse to buy milk.
   c)   Drain the orange juice carton and put it back in the fridge.
8.   You and your spouse find that you have a free Saturday night. You....
   a)   Hire a babysitter and go out for dinner and a movie.
   b)   Order pizza and eat it together.
   c)   Go to your separate rooms to watch TV.
9.   It snowed last night and there's a foot of snow on the driveway. You....
   a)   Go out and shovel the snow so your spouse won't be late for work.
   b)   Back the car through the snow leaving the shovelling for your better half.
   c)   Turn off the alarm and go back to sleep.
10.   Your spouse expresses sexual interest but you have a headache. You....
   a)   Forget about your headache and make love to your spouse.
   b)   Say "Not tonight, dear, I have a headache."
   c)   Say "Stop touching me, you're giving me a headache!"

Scoring - Give yourself one point for each a) answer, three points for each b) answer and five points for each c). Total up your score and determine what range you fall within.

<u>Less than 20</u>: You're a perfect poster guy or gal for the pop psychologists. In other words, you're a sad excuse for a human being and need help urgently. Your incessant need to please and your constant search for approval will only cause you and those around you great stress.

<u>20 to 40</u>: You show signs of achieving true mediocrity but there's work yet to be done. Stop worrying about others and take care of your own needs. Some may call you selfish but I'll just call you average.

<u>More than 40</u>: Congratulations! You're exceedingly average and probably don't spend an extra minute a day worrying about your relationship or your emotional I.Q. Keep up the good work and steer clear of the pop psych wizards.

<u>More than 50</u>: You're probably a normal, average person when it comes to relationships but you obviously need some remedial work in Grade 2 arithmetic.

"To sleep, perchance to dream"
The Toronto Star   February 5, 1999

My wife Cheryl is a big believer in the power of dreams. She's one of those people who keeps a journal and records her nighttime visions faithfully. To her, dreams are filled with portents and fortuitous omens.

I, on the other hand, view things differently. It's not that I don't believe in dreams; it's just that I interpret them in my own way.

For example, my wife recently dreamed that I was wearing a new suit and was surrounded by mahogany. She interpreted that to mean that I got a promotion, a new desk and a big salary increase. I interpreted it to mean that I'd just been laid out in a casket.

On one occasion, my wife had a vision that there was a shiny black car in the driveway. She took that to mean that we were soon going to be the proud owners of a fancy new automobile. I wasn't so sure.

Well, it turns out that Cheryl was half right. A few weeks later, my old clunker died and I bought a shiny black car. Unfortunately it was six years old and was about to blow its head gasket. The only shiny black thing left in the driveway after that was a large pool of motor oil.

My wife claims that her dreams tap into the collective unconscious - that common well of spirit described by people like C.G. Jung. I, on the other hand, subscribe to the theory of
the individual unconscious - i.e. - the clueless, selfish little id that hides inside my head and asks for things.

That's why I view dreams differently. When my wife has a vision that we're all flying on a jet, she assumes it means we're going on an exotic vacation. I assume it simply means that she wants to go on an exotic vacation. In my mind, if her dream comes to fruition at all, it will likely be in the form of a rain-drenched one-week trip to Disney World in a charter plane with eleven-inch seats.

Now some might say that the only difference here is that Cheryl's an optimist and I'm a pessimist. That's probably true, but it doesn't change my belief in the meaning of dreams. If you dream it then you likely fear it, hate it or want it. But I doubt that it means you're necessarily going to get it.

Well, you say, what about those instances where someone

dreams of an event that later actually occurs? Well, what about it? With five billion people having several dreams a night, odds are that one or two of them might actually be realized. Yet you don't hear a lot about the billions of others that don't come true.

Now I'm not saying there's nothing to this dreaming business. After all, dreams must serve some purpose. But I doubt that it goes much beyond simply letting off some psychic steam. In other words, it's better that I dream about punching my boss in the nose rather than actually doing it.

As with most things, however, I've hedged my bets. If Cheryl is right, I sure don't want to miss out on all those benefits when her visions do start coming true. So even while I play the skeptic by day, I still have a little bit of faith at night. That's why I sometimes whisper those magic words into Cheryl's sleeping ear: "Big-screen TV."

"Dog days"
The Ottawa Citizen August 20, 2005

I like dogs. I really do. I just don't want to live with one.

After years of endless lobbying by my wife and daughter, I finally relented and agreed to get a dog. Since my wife Cheryl is allergic to canines, our choice of breeds was limited. But after much research, Cheryl and Sarah settled on a Portuguese Water Dog, a non-shedding breed that I assumed, from its name, would be happier in Halifax or Rio de Janeiro than in landlocked Ottawa.

Despite my reservations (after all, the PWD is described as a medium to large-sized dog), Cheryl put down a deposit with a breeder for one of the puppies from a recent litter. Little did I know, this was just the beginning of an ongoing series of dog-related financial outlays.

The puppy himself cost Cheryl $1700, an amount that served to immediately dilate my pupils to their maximum aperture. And, of course, there were expenditures on high-end crates, bowls, toys, treats and food.

But that was only the beginning. As with any new arrival, it's necessary to baby-proof the house. That meant baby gates for each of the three entrances to the kitchen.

It also meant a new $800 Afghan rug to cover the five steps to the upper level. Although I'd been climbing them for years with my arthritic hips, apparently dogs shouldn't be walking up hardwood steps. Something about bone development and possible hip dysplasia.

Not only did the house have to be properly prepared for our new pet. The backyard had to be brought up to standard, too. That meant $300 for a gate and the purchase of assorted pieces of wood to block any escape routes under and around the fence.

I didn't recall such elaborate preparations for Sarah's arrival nine years earlier. As I remember it, poor Sarah had to make do with a secondhand crib, dresser and change table and a small throw rug from Walmart. Then again, we hadn't paid $1700 for her.

Finally, D-day arrived. Cheryl and Sarah headed out one recent Saturday morning and returned that afternoon with a cute, black and white ball of fur that Sarah had christened Oreo.

Since I was the only reluctant prospective dog owner in the

family, I was repeatedly asked if I liked Oreo which, of course, I did. As I said, I like dogs. And who could resist an adorable, black and white puppy even if he did bite, chew and pee at will?

What I didn't like were the changes that Oreo brought with him. For years, I could make a quick trip from our living room to the rec room in the basement. Not anymore.

Now that same trip involves stepping over one baby gate, navigating a makeshift extra step and undoing and re-hitching a second gate. And if I forget to bring something, I have to repeat the entire process two more times.

At one point, I sensed that Cheryl was sympathizing with my new plight. Especially when she asked if I had any problems with the new makeshift step. When I said it wasn't too bad and thanks for thinking of me, she said that she wasn't asking for my sake but wanted to know if it would be OK for Oreo.

Cheryl had earlier informed me that from Oreo's perspective, she was dominant and thus qualified as the so-called alpha bitch. After her somewhat insensitive comment about the step, I was tempted to concur in that observation but ultimately thought better of it.

Which was just as well since, contrary to expectations, my predicted role as the alpha male was not coming to fruition. Oreo seemed to pay no more deference or respect to me than he did to the kitchen floor which was quickly becoming his preferred voiding area.

Instead, I was rapidly descending our household hierarchy and apparently destined for the number four position. At that point, I was just thankful that we didn't have a gerbil or a hamster to compete with for the penultimate rung on the family ladder.

Despite the new inconveniences, the lifestyle changes and my many misgivings, things progressed fairly well. Oreo didn't have any long, whiny nights and he adjusted fairly quickly to his new home. Who knows? Perhaps he is a discriminating puppy and appreciated that we had provided him with the best in dog bowls and high-end, Afghan stair carpeting.

But the expenses continue. $135 for the first vet visit. $250 for five sessions with a dog trainer who I suspect is training us, not the dog. And an unspecified future outlay for enrollment in doggie obedience school.

I'd like to say that it's all been worth it, that Oreo is one priceless, lovable puppy. But I'm not quite at that stage yet. Hopefully some day I'll be as attached to him as he appears to be to my pant leg and slippers.

"The Kama Sutra of Housework"
The Smithsonian Magazine   December 2007

> Men are beginning to understand that doing housework...unprompted goes a long way to creating marital happiness....Intimacy is not just for the bedroom, in other words. Foreplay can begin with a dish towel.
> —The Toronto Globe and Mail

Thus follows the Kama Sutra of Domestic Love:

On the Use of Outside Help
In an effort to enhance domestic congress, some couples may seek the services of one professionally trained in the art. However, this is seldom as satisfying as when the man performs the task alone. But in the interest of matrimonial harmony, if both the man and the woman work outside the home, it is acceptable to engage a cleaning person once every two weeks.

The Washing of Dishes
The woman submerges her dishes in warm, soapy water, rinses them in clear water and passes them to the man. The man employs a slow, clockwise motion to dry them thoroughly with a dish towel. After about 20 minutes, the solicitous partner will switch roles for variety.

On Doing Laundry
The man is often too hurried and wishes to place the clothes immediately in the washing machine. He must learn patience and be guided by the woman, who will teach him the art of sorting and, in time, even to pre-soak. The slow, deliberate dividing of clothing into piles of whites, lights and colors will lighten the loads and heighten the pleasure.

The Art of the Dryer
Once the man has mastered the washing routine, he can be introduced to the dryer. Again, he must act against his nature and learn patience before inserting damp garments into the cylinder. Although all items can be placed into the dryer, he must learn to withhold some of them. What could be a most pleasurable cycle can

end in anger and disappointment for the woman if a delicate undergarment is shredded or blue jeans are shrunk.

On Extracting Dirt from the Carpet

This is an uncommon task for a man. Before he can perform the act he must first be alerted to the existence of dirt in the carpet. Once introduced to the vacuum cleaner, its mechanical nature may overexcite him and cause him to proceed with inappropriate haste. The woman must also ensure that he is schooled in which attachment to use for each task.

The Cleaning of the Bathroom

Most men are unfamiliar with this delicate maneuver and may initially resist. A woman should not expect too much at first, taking initial satisfaction from the man's cursory sponging of the sink and tub before he advances to the washing of the floor and the polishing of taps. Be aware that he will not readily clean the bowl. But if a wise woman knows how to reward her mate, she may never have to use a toilet brush again.

"Husband Instruction Manual"
The Christian Science Monitor
September 22, 2008

Congratulations on the acquisition of your brand new 2008 husband. You have chosen the best that modern biology has to offer in the way of life partners. While your 2008 husband is built to last a lifetime, these care and handling instructions will help you get the most out of your man.

Laundry instructions

Although we have implemented many improvements in this year's model (e.g. - automatic toilet seat replacement, limited childcare abilities, expectoration and flatulence control), we have not yet perfected an automatic self-laundering option. Thus, you must repeatedly remind your husband to pick up his dirty clothes, sort his laundry by color and wash appropriate-sized loads. Some owners have found it easier to simply perform these functions themselves.

Dressing instructions

Most husbands come with only two wardrobe options: work and casual. Therefore please ensure that you assist your husband in any clothing purchases in order to avoid nasty fashion surprises. As in past years, the 2008 husband has pre-set fashion preferences which may clash with your taste. To date, we have yet to perfect an acceptable "color sense" module although the deluxe accessory package does include a formalwear option for occasional use. WARNING: Constant wardrobe monitoring is strongly recommended especially on weekends. Repeated exposure to baggy sweat pants and hole-filled t-shirts may void the warranty.

Cooking instructions

If you chose the deluxe accessory package, you can count on your husband to successfully cook meals on his own for many years to come. The standard model, on the other hand, has few kitchen skills and a limited cuisine. Unless you're willing to invest the time necessary to train your husband in the culinary arts, don't expect much beyond making toast and boiling water. However, all models do come equipped with the outdoor barbecue function.

Listening instructions
Despite years of research, we have not yet been able to produce a husband who really listens. Wives are free to urge their spouses to listen and "express their feelings" but we can offer no guarantees that you will achieve any meaningful results. Through persistent effort, some customers have trained their husbands to adopt a semi-satisfying simulated listening posture.

Fitness instructions
Your 2008 husband is properly proportioned and in good shape. However, in order to retain that shape and those proportions, you must insist on a strict regimen of daily exercise and a healthy diet. Failure to keep your husband active and eating properly will often result in a sluggish spouse with a widening waistline and a sagging seat. WARNING: Do not rely on in-home exercise equipment and always ration beer, pizza and chips carefully.

Romance instructions
Although the listening capabilities of the 2008 husband are limited, he does possess excellent eyesight. Thus, in order to activate the romance function, emphasize visual stimuli. Sophisticated conversational and emotional skills are still not available on the 2008 husband although our genetic engineers hope to have an improved product ready by the next millennium.

LIMITED WARRANTY: Our 2008 husband is guaranteed against defects in workmanship for ninety (90) days. If, for any reason, you wish to return your husband during the warranty period, we will issue a full refund but only if he is returned in his original packaging. After that, you're on your own.

CHAPTER SIX

VACATIONS

"The diary of a winter getaway"
The Chicago Tribune   November 30, 2003

It's that time of the year again. And, no, we're not talking about eating Thanksgiving leftovers or shopping for Christmas presents. Brace yourself: It's time to plan your big getaway from the soon-to-be frozen north. Here's how one escapee's trip proceeded last winter.

Fall 2002: Advance book one week Caribbean holiday for March break to ensure reservation at preferred "family oriented" resort and to get 9:30 a.m. departure time for flight.

January 2003: Take out second mortgage to pay for trip.

March 3: Pick up tickets and discover charter airline has changed departure time to 6:30 a.m. and requires passengers to arrive three hours early.

March 6: Set three alarm clocks for 3, 3:05 and 3:10 a.m. Seven-year-old daughter Sarah falls asleep at 8:30 p.m. Try to sleep at 9 p.m. Take pharmaceutical product. Wake up at 11 p.m.

March 7: Finally get up at 2:30 a.m. and turn off first alarm clock. Get dressed, check house, wake Sarah at 3 a.m. Scare entire family as 3:05 alarm clock goes off and again when 3:10 alarm clock goes off. Call for taxi. Eat breakfast. Stumble into taxi with seven bags for one-week trip.

4 a.m.: Arrive at airport in minus 4 Fahrenheit weather. Load luggage cart to top and perform treacherous slalom through various roped off rows. Check in five largest pieces of luggage. Give thanks not able to afford two-week getaway.

4:30 a.m.: Finish check-in and stand in line at airport doughnut shop for much-needed coffee and box of non-metaphysical doughnut holes. Realize two hours left until plane departs. Vow to ignore early arrival warnings for future vacations, if any.

6 a.m.: Board flight. Discover charter seat size has shrunk since last Caribbean flight in previous century. Luckily assigned aisle seat allowing stretching of left leg into aisle to assist rapid deceleration of beverage cart.

6:45 a.m.: Plane departs. Passengers applaud. Wonder about appropriate response if plane fails to leave ground.

Noon: Plane lands in small Caribbean airport. More applause.

2 p.m.: Luggage arrives at terminal. Apparently traveled on separate plane. Probably had more leg room.

4 p.m.: Arrive at all-inclusive resort only to discover functioning toilet and working air conditioner apparently not included in package.

6 p.m.: Dine at all-inclusive buffet restaurant featuring authentic local cuisine tailored to primarily American clientele. Enjoy "special" meal of hamburgesa, papas fritas and bisteca.

7 p.m.: Daughter insists on joining other kids at games and movie night on the beach. Enjoy romantic evening alone with wife by falling asleep watching movie on HBO.

10 p.m.: Go to pick up tearful daughter who was distraught at our absence. Daughter vows never to go to Kids' Club again, thereby negating primary advantage of "family oriented" resort.

10:30 p.m.: Sarah sound asleep. Wife and self wide awake as "genuine Vegas-style" stage show starts outside our building followed by Hades-style argument by couple in next room.

March 8: Sarah awakes at 6 a.m. and rouses Mom and Dad from four-hour reverie.

Noon: Enjoy "native" lunch of perro caliente, nachos and pizza after relaxing morning in sun by the pool.

4 p.m.: Realize that sunscreen only used on daughter. Begin week-long impression of human lobster.

7 p.m.: Enjoy "special" dinner on the beach including "special" garnish of windblown sand.

10 p.m.: Sarah in second hour of sleep as wife and self lie in bed anxiously awaiting start of "Broadway-style" musical revue outside balcony followed by round two of arguing neighbors from Hell.

March 9 and 10: (See March 8.)

March 11: In hopes of achieving full night's sleep, ask for room change at noon.

3 p.m.: Room change completed. Now on second floor facing "quiet" adults-only pool. Visions of restful sleep bring joy to frazzled nerves.

9 p.m.: Retire for expected quiet night. Sarah asleep in five minutes; wife and self five minutes later.

9:30 p.m.: Awakened by Caribbean band at adults' pool celebrating "special" Caribbean night. Give up and tune in to "Smokey and the Bandit III" on HBO.

March 12: (See March 11.)

March 13: Spend much of day bargaining with beach vendors for "genuine" souvenirs for family, friends and schoolmates back home. Vendors sense last-minute air of desperation and accept only American currency and refuse to lower prices.

March 14: Up early for 8 a.m. checkout and 8:30 a.m. bus ride to airport for 1:30 p.m. departure. Apparently Caribbean airport security tighter than U.S./Canadian version notwithstanding thatched roof and open-air design.

9 a.m.: Arrive at airport, check in and clear security in 30 minutes, leaving four hours to explore world's smallest airport and duty-free shop featuring 20 brands of cigars and 30 varieties of rum.

1:30 p.m.: Plane departs.

6 p.m.: Plane lands during snowstorm. Once again, passengers applaud. Make mental note to check airline's safety record.

8 p.m.: Having located most of our luggage, hail taxi for final leg of journey.

8:30 p.m.: Arrive home to snowed-in driveway and 5-degree Fahrenheit temperature. Enjoy first full night of sleep in eight days. Start planning next restful March break in Caribbean setting.

"A Week in the Cottage"
The Ottawa Citizen   August 19, 2004

Whether you own one, borrow one or rent one, a stay at a lakeside cottage is a mandatory summer pastime. It's as Canadian as ice skating and Royal commissions.

Since we neither inherited a cottage nor the windfall needed to buy one, we fall into the category of renters. Each year, we pay someone else for the privilege of staying at their rustic retreat. The grating fact that we are contributing to someone else's mortgage payments is balanced by the satisfying knowledge that we don't have to worry about roofs, docks and septic systems.

Each summer, our family looks forward to a relaxing week lounging in the sun and enjoying the quiet sounds of the great outdoors. This summer, we figured we were guaranteed more of the same by booking the second week of August. After all, if there's any summer in Canada, it can definitely be found in early August.

Not this year, it turns out. In a country marked by ten months of winter and two months of tough sledding, God apparently decided to punish us even more. Hence, what was to be our week at the cottage turned out instead to be a week *in* the cottage.

Our seven-day stay had an auspicious beginning. An iffy Sunday was followed by an absolutely gorgeous Monday: a sunny 26 degrees Celsius day with hardly a cloud in the sky. It looked like we had indeed picked the perfect week.

But Tuesday was the exception that drowned the rule. It rained and it rained and it rained some more. Tuesday morning was spent playing a marathon game of Monopoly on a game board that appeared to be older than the cottage. Tuesday afternoon was filled with rental movies. And Tuesday evening found two adults and two children barely tolerating one another's presence in cramped quarters.

Tuesday night was spent in prayer. Prayer that the weather forecast was wrong. Prayer not so much for sunny, warm days but rather a more modest prayer simply for no rain.

Our prayers were only partially answered. Wednesday was definitely better than Tuesday. It only rained half the day. Not only did that mean less Monopoly and fewer movies. It also meant one canoe ride and a brief swim.

Wednesday night was spent discussing Thursday's weather forecast. What exactly did "cloudy with a 60% probability of precipitation" signify? Did that mean we had a 40% chance of no rain? No one knew for sure.

The sun rose early Thursday morning. Not that we would have known. Dogged by cloud cover that would have made St. John's proud, we traded stories of bygone sunny days and waited for the inevitable rain.

As the others risked a brief canoe ride, I drove into the nearby village to return our supply of sunscreen and invest the refund in more movie rentals. And not a moment too soon. By the time I got back to the cottage, the skies had opened leaving three drenched canoeists huddled around the TV begging for entertainment.

As the rain continued, we coped as best we could. Movies, books and board games. These were the new companions of our week in the cottage. Luckily for us, this cottage was well equipped. Not only could we play Monopoly, we also had the option of Scrabble, Clue and the appropriately named Trouble.

Friday brought an end to the rain. Sadly, it also brought a cold front with a high of 17 degrees. After breakfast, I loaded up the VCR and started the wood stove to take the chill out of the August air.

Leaving the rest huddled around the TV, I retreated to the bedroom to read. If this was to be the sunless summer, I figured that at least I could indulge myself with a nature book or two. And that's how I spent the rest of the day - reading about the great outdoors that I was apparently doomed to experience only secondhand.

Saturday was our departure day. As you might expect, the clouds slowly dissipated throughout the morning leaving a bright, sunny, warm day that was perfect for everything except packing and cleaning. By the time we loaded up the car, the temperature had risen to 25 degrees and the sun was shining through the trees in a mocking farewell.

Despite the rain, the clouds and the cold, our week *in* the cottage was almost as good as a week at the cottage. Whether it's sunbathing or enforced reading, swimming or Monopoly marathons, nature hikes or rainy day naps, time at a cottage takes you away from the everyday routine and helps recharge the psychic batteries. Unless, of course, your psychic batteries are solar powered. Then it might help to have some sun.

"A Timeshare Romance"
Stitches Magazine   February, 1999

It was our first time. After ten years of togetherness, my wife and I finally decided to take the plunge. We are now no longer timeshare virgins.

Like so many romances, it started with a phone call. An anonymous suitor lured us with an offer of two nights accommodation at a luxury resort for a fraction of the regular cost. And all we had to do was agree to attend a 90 minute presentation.

Our innate skepticism led us initially to say no. But after some thought, we realized we could tack those two nights on to another resort stay we had already booked thereby extending our vacation.

What's the harm, I thought. Just because a guy buys you dinner, you don't have to....... Well, you get the picture.

A two-hour drive brought us to our destination. It was all that our suitor promised and more. A one-bedroom hotel suite with all the amenities was ours for two nights.

We swam in the pool, relaxed in the whirlpool and watched a movie uninterrupted as our two-and-a-half-year-old daughter slept in the bedroom. It was heavenly.

The next day, we took in some of the sights and then put in some serious relaxing time at the pool. We'd almost forgotten about our afternoon date.

At 3 o'clock, we headed off for the presentation. Our daughter was placed in a daycare area which she took to right away. We thought about signing up for a second presentation.

After coffee and snacks, we met our date who I'll call Steve (because that was his name). He asked us to join him at a window side table and we engaged in the casual give and take of first time acquaintances.

Steve was good; he was very good. He skilfully elicited all kinds of information from us before telling us about himself and his company. I started to feel something special happening.

My wife was more skeptical and reticent than me. But once Steve started weaving his magic visions of timeshare vacations around the world, she, too, started to fall under his spell.

And when we finally left the window side table and visited the one-bedroom condo that would be ours forever if we just said yes, both our heads were swimming. I'm not the kind of guy to say yes on the first date, but this seemed like the real thing.

After the tour, we headed back to Steve's place which was a small enclosed office. Steve started quoting prices and points and transfer options and it all sounded confusing but wonderful. This year in Mexico, next year in Hawaii and maybe Morocco the following year.

Our resistance was still there but it was waning. And then Steve started offering bonuses and incentives one after the other. A free week here, free add-ons there, inexpensive getaways - it sounded too good to be true.

But all this would only be ours if we said yes today. We couldn't wait for a second date; we had to do it now.

Steve left us alone in his room to think about it. After we caught our breath, my wife and I realized that we weren't yet ready for a whirlwind romance like this. We liked Steve but we hardly knew him.

So we called Steve back and broke the news to him. Considering all he'd done for us, he took it well. In fact, he even acknowledged that he knew pretty much from the start that I wasn't that kind of guy.

We parted on good terms and Steve even said to look him up if we were ever in town again. But despite the headiness of that first date and though that timeshare property is probably a great deal for some lucky couple out there, I knew that we'd never see Steve again.

"Family Camp 17"
Stitches Magazine   May, 2000

I recently tried a new form of torture called family camping. For a modest fee, my wife and I and our three and a half year old daughter spent three days in a rustic camp located on a small mountain lake. It sounded like an idyllic getaway. It ended up being a living nightmare.

Our first evening at Family Camp 17 consisted mostly of learning the 316 camp rules. Rule Number One: "If in doubt, don't do it." I asked if there was any rule against getting in my car and leaving. No one seemed amused.

We were also informed that the camp's clocks were turned back an hour, ostensibly to give us more "fun time" in the evening hours. I soon came to suspect, however, that it was done to disorient us and keep us compliant and submissive.

Meals were at 8, 12 and 5:30 sharp and consisted of setting up tables, chairs and plates and madly rushing for the kitchen window to grab trays of food. Camp veterans grabbed two trays of everything leaving rookies like us with slim pickings. I ate every meal like it was my last.

The first night was an omen of things to come. It was unusually hot and humid and I tossed and turned on sweat-soaked bedding until 4 A.M. when the loudest thunderstorm I had ever experienced passed overhead and knocked out the power. When my daughter crawled into bed with me at 5:30 A.M., I accepted that I was not going to sleep that night.

As I staggered out of bed that first morning, it dawned on me that without electricity I would not be able to shower and shave. Then again, it seemed only fitting that I should look as horrible as I felt.

Despite the power outage, we were still fed. Breakfast comprised bread and butter and cold cereal and milk and lunch consisted of cold sandwiches and a grape Kool-Aid concoction eerily reminiscent of Jonestown.

That afternoon, the power returned. As campers dispersed to various scheduled activities, I snuck back to our cabin and luxuriated in a hot shower and the thought of a nap. The shower I got; the nap I didn't. Despite the wealth of activities, my eleven-year-old nephew and his friend decided to stay in the cabin all afternoon playing board games. Their raucous banter killed my pathetic attempt at sleep.

After a hot supper, we waited for the evening activity which consisted of singing songs around a lakeside bonfire. Everyone seemed to enjoy it including the bugs which attacked me relentlessly.

I desperately hoped for a night of sleep but, of course, that was not to be. Although the temperature dropped, I was now able to focus on the secondary reason I couldn't sleep the night before: the bed.

The bed was a narrow wooden contraption stuck between two walls and covered with a mattress that was as thin as it was uncomfortable. As I rotated from hip to hip, I longed for pharmaceuticals to put me to sleep.

The next morning, I convinced my wife that our three night stay should be reduced to two. The only problem was how to break out of Family Camp 17.

I tactfully informed the camp director that we would be leaving one day early. She informed me that there would be an extra $25 charge. Little did she know that I would have paid ten times that amount to escape.

We quickly packed our bags and left before the director changed her mind. And with awe-inspiring celerity, we sped home where I luxuriated in a warm bath and a firm bed.

I've learned my lesson - family camping is not for me. If I have to suffer sleepless nights and bug-infested days, I'd rather not pay for the privilege.

"Do Come to Our Cottage"
Stitches Magazine   September, 2003

Dear Friends,

As you know, we spend much of the summer at our rustic cottage on Rabid Dog Island in the middle of picturesque Rocky Marsh Lake. Because of your past generosity in having us over for dinner, taking us to a show or sharing time at your ski condo, we'd like to extend an invitation to you to come and stay at our cottage this summer.

We don't have a phone but feel free to drop by any time. Just remember to bring your own sleeping bags and a tent as the cottage is a bit small and there may not be enough room for everybody on the fold out cots. Bring plenty of food and drink, too, as we don't have a refrigerator since there's no electricity.

Although not an absolute necessity, bug repellant, toilet paper and a flashlight are strongly recommended. In past years, some guests have felt it necessary to bring rat poison or mouse traps. We're happy to report that our family of fury friends has all but disappeared this summer thanks to our new friends Mr. Raccoon and Mrs. Skunk.

Don't worry about sunscreen. We've got plenty at the cottage although it's doubtful you'll have to use it. It's been a wet summer so far and the long range forecast is for more. However, don't forget your books, playing cards and board games. There's nothing like the communal fun of a non-stop Monopoly marathon on a rainy day or two.

That reminds us. Don't forget rainwear, tarps for your tent and a small shovel to dig a trench. When you're wet you're wet, of course, but at least you won't get soaked.

Now for directions. Take the I-90 north for four hours to Exit 16 (No Man's Exit). Take Highway 12A (not 12B!!) going east (if you pass Harry's Gun Rack and Lawn Ornament Emporium, you've taken the wrong road).

After about twenty miles, you'll see a burned out barn on your right. Just past the barn there's a gravel road called Dead Man's Road. Turn left and go about 43 miles. Just after the gravel turns to dirt, there's a small lane to the right. Don't take that lane. Instead keep going on the dirt road for about 19 miles (Did we mention to gas up at Exit 16?). You'll see a house with three rusted out cars in the yard and a 1978 Ford pickup in the driveway.

Turn into the driveway which leads to a narrow dirt road beyond the property. Don't be afraid of the Rottweiler. He's usually chained up. If he's not, just make sure your windows are rolled up and that you have lots of windshield washer fluid.

Take the dirt road about five miles to a fork in the road. Keep left and after about two miles you should come to Lost Explorer Lake. Park your car next to the storage shed. You'll find the key under the third painted rock on your right.

Open up the storage shed and remove the canoe and life jackets. Lock the shed and replace the key. You're almost here!

Load your provisions in the canoe and put on the life jackets. Head east on Lost Explorer Lake. After about an hour, you'll see a small stream. Land the canoe, empty your provisions and start a brief portage.

Follow the orange markers on the trees for about two miles and you should find Rocky Marsh Lake. Load up again and continue paddling east. Rocky Marsh Lake is a surprisingly long lake but you should see our island in less than two hours. If you don't, check with one of the three other cottagers on the lake for directions.

When you see the broken dock and the marshy beach surrounded by rocks, you'll know you've made it to Rabid Dog Island. Climb the 96 steps (watch out for numbers 26, 46 and 91) and knock on the door.

If we're not in, help yourself to whatever you need. We're probably just out hiking or fishing. Or we may be away on our annual one-month trip to Provence. If so, we'll see you in the fall.

Have fun!

The Longworths (Sally & Sid)

P.S. - Don't drink the lake water unless you've boiled it for at least ten minutes. And feel free to use all the powdered milk and oatmeal you want, assuming Mr. Raccoon or Mrs. Skunk haven't already helped themselves.

CHAPTER SEVEN

HEALTH, DIET AND EXERCISE

"Sweet Dreams, the Twinkie Diet"
The Chicago Tribune   January 28, 2004

"The Twinkies Diet," by Dr. David Martin, E.D. (doctor of eatology)

Isn't it amazing? We can send a man to the moon and put another Texan in the White House but we can't come up with a simple way to lose weight.   That's because, until now, no one has satisfactorily explained the eating process.

One diet suggests it's all dependent on blood type. Another says it's a question of maintaining a high-fat, high-protein, low-carbohydrate regime. Still another claims the secret is when and how you combine your foods.

But none of these approaches really makes much sense. The simple answer is that food is our body's fuel. And like a powerful missile, the best food is nature's high energy rocket fuel: sugar.

That's right. Sugar is a high-energy carbohydrate that delivers the biggest metabolic bang for the buck. It's quickly processed by the body and, just like rocket fuel, is converted to straight power. Plus, it tastes great.   We've tested sugar on patients at our lab and found that a high-sugar, low-protein, low-nutrient regimen helps satisfy those nasty diet-related cravings. It also helps patients stay on their diet plan with much less effort. Surprisingly, the compliance rate in our studies approached 100 percent.

It is still too early to evaluate average weight loss on the sugar diet. Preliminary results suggest that during the first few weeks there may actually be a slight weight gain in some patients. But it is expected that, over time, the well-known "rebound" effect will activate, thereby initiating the so-called "fat-burning" phase.

Based on our results to date, we recommend the following daily regime:

<u>Breakfast</u>: 1 cup of coffee with 3 spoons of sugar1 bowl of sweetened cereal with chocolate milk or 2 4-ounce doughnuts or pastries (remember--white flour is quickly converted by your body to--you guessed it--sugar)

<u>Morning snack</u>: 1 chocolate bar or suitable substitute (e.g. hard candies, Twizzlers, etc.) (as needed)

<u>Lunch</u>: 1 cup of coffee with 4 spoons of sugar (no dairy, if possible) or 1 large soft drink (no diet drinks, please)1 box of doughnut holes or 2 Twinkies1 cup or cone of ice cream

<u>Afternoon snack</u>: 1 small bag of cookies with creamy centers (as needed)

<u>Dinner</u>: 1 cup of coffee with 4 spoons of sugar or 1 large soft drink (may substitute beer or dessert wine)1 small black forest cake or 1/2 fruit pie or 1/4 baked Alaska1 small box of assorted chocolates for dessert

<u>Evening snack</u>: 1 small container of Haagen-Dazs ice cream or (as needed) 1 bottle of "Dr. Martin's Sucrose Sports Drink"

As with any lifestyle change, it may be difficult to achieve 100 percent compliance all the time. We don't expect that. We realize that almost everyone will occasionally have cravings for other foods. That's normal.

The key is not to become too rigid. If you have a craving for fruit, go ahead and have some. Remember, fruits have sugar too. A kind of sugar called fructose. And don't forget; you can always choose a candied fruit.

Rest assured that the Twinkies Diet will work for you. This "medical breakthrough" is the result of the application of the latest scientific techniques in an environment of professionalism and objectivity. For example, our double-blind studies were carried out with no direct financial assistance from the sugar industry.

As with most independent scientific research, however, it is often difficult to get adequate funding. Thus we gratefully acknowledge the free supplies of sweets donated by various manufacturers. And we also appreciate the all-expenses paid trip for two to Hawaii and the kind offer of lifetime employment at the Sugar Council.

Together we can make a difference.

"Nasty, Brutish and Short"
The Ottawa Citizen   March 21, 2002

My face was planted squarely in the snow, my arms were lying uselessly by my sides and my feet were splayed in opposite directions. Once again, I was enjoying that great Canadian winter pastime: cross-country skiing.

Fifteen years ago, I took my first stab at this so-called sport. I rented a pair of ancient skis and boots and headed off to ski the back forty on a friend's eastern Ontario farm.

That outing symbolized what was to become more an ongoing dialectical discourse (thesis - antithesis - twisted ankle) than an enjoyable recreation. Half way into the woods, the rubber protrusion on the front of my aging right ski boot tore off leaving me stranded in deep snow at the furthest point from the farmhouse. Luckily, the owner rescued me from my ignominious fate with his snowmobile.

But I would not allow this setback to defeat me. I am nothing if not stubborn. Actually, I am nothing if not stupid. Deceived by the apparent simplicity of cross-country skiing, I purchased my own set of skis and boots.

Cross-country skiing for me is an adventure. Not in the way it is for most people - i.e. - a meditative discovery of the joys and beauties of the winter wonderland that is Canada. For me, the adventure is simply whether I will make it back to the car without serious injury.

In the decade and a half that I have owned skis, I have used them on average twice a winter. That works out to about thirty outings. At an average 4.5 falls per outing, I figure I've wiped out a grand total of 135 times. Counting the occasional accident just getting the skis and poles in and out of the car, I'm probably up to an even 140 falls.

Hills are no great problem for me. I simply ski down them, fall diagonally face first into the snow, pick myself up and carry on.

Icy patches, too, receive consistent treatment. I plant my poles firmly in the snow as my skis shoot rapidly backwards leaving me face down kissing the ice with my arms perilously entwined in the ski poles.

And ski waxing? Don't get me started! I have a collection of little cylindrical containers large enough to make a giant votive candle to pray for guidance on which type of wax to use on any given day.

Now, why, you might ask, do I persist in this clearly painful pastime when I don't have to? The answer has something to do with winter and something to do with religion.

Because Canadian winters are longer than the average computer warranty, I feel compelled to take part in at least some outdoor activities not involving snow shovels. I'm not so foolish as to take up downhill skiing at my age. Therefore, that leaves me with skating and cross-country skiing.

As for the theological aspect, I now realize that my commitment to slow-speed planking owes much to religion. For me, cross-country skiing is less an amusing diversion and more a Calvinist recreation. In other words, the object of the exercise is not to have fun but rather to subject myself to the travails of nature as a metaphor for the harshness of life.

My occasional handicapped treks through the snow are a stark reminder of the Hobbesian view of life - i.e. - nasty, brutish and short. Like banging your head against the wall, it just feels so darn good when you stop.

So I will persist in this medieval self-flagellation that is known as cross-country skiing. It allows me to pretend that I have come to terms with winter, that I somehow have achieved a detente of sorts with this hellish season. And on that rare occasion when the snow has just fallen, the sun is out and I've miraculously chosen the right ski wax, it's actually even fun.

"All This Exercising"
The Toronto Star   September 2, 1998

I'm a baby boomer. In fact, I'm probably the quintessential baby boomer. Born in 1950, I've managed to acquire two degrees, a house, a wife and 1.2 kids.

Part of being a baby boomer is exercising. And I'm no exception. For years now, I've been working out in a vain attempt to maintain health and avoid injury. First I played squash until my ankles and knees gave out. Then I tried high impact aerobics until my hips wore out. Now I'm into step aerobics but I figure it's only a matter of time before some other part of my anatomy gives way.

If you're starting to see a pattern here, so am I. Each of my efforts to improve my health has inevitably and inexorably led to the further decline of my body. And I'm not alone as my boomer contemporaries and I exercise our bodies into the ground. At the rate I'm going, I expect that in ten years or so I'll be an avid participant in what's sure to be the boomer obsession of the new millennium - wheel chair weightlifting.

Luckily, for me, my local fitness club has looked into the future and designed a whole new exercise program for us aging boomers. It's called Lazy Boy Plus and I think my generation will embrace it with the zealotry we previously reserved for tie-dyed clothes and disco dancing.

My bi-weekly class takes place in a small exercise room with several rows of rocker-recliners facing the instructor's chair on an elevated platform. The warmup session consists of adjusting the chair into the various positions from upright to supine and repeating the cycle several times. Then we move into the cardio portion of the workout which consists of a wide variety of movements designed to keep our bodies functioning well into our fifties.

First we practice the use of the TV remote control from various positions and angles. Next, we recline the chair and roll from side to side. Then we raise the recliner, get out of the chair and circle it five times thereby simulating a trip to the kitchen for snacks. Half pound weights in each hand can be used to substitute for a beer and a sandwich. At my club, we've taken to using the real things.

When we've returned to our chairs, we recline them again and practice various stretching maneuvers. There's the stretch to the right to reach the beer or sandwich. There's the stretch to the left to reach the adjusting mechanism on the side of the chair. And there's the stretch to the center to look for any potato chips that may have fallen on the floor. And finally there's the stretch to the back or what we've come to call the pre-nap stretch. As our instructor notes, these movements should be alternated to avoid overdeveloping the muscles on any one side.

Like any good exercise program, Lazy Boy Plus has a cool down period as well. But unlike those other programs that require actual exertion during this phase of the workout, Lazy Boy Plus only asks that you stretch out fully in the rocker recliner for five minutes with your eyes closed. If you happen to fall asleep, all the better.

Lazy Boy Plus is also very adaptable. Instead of using the TV remote control, you can substitute a cordless phone. Or for those so inclined, computer mouse movements can be added. And for the truly ambitious, there's even LB+ circuit training where you move from chair to chair during the workout.

No more weights, no more steps and no more machines. With Lazy Boy Plus, you may never feel the burn again. But, believe me, you won't miss it. And no more worries about the dangers of high impact aerobics. Exercise programs don't come any lower impact than Lazy Boy Plus.

I'm eternally thankful for this new approach to working out. I was afraid I'd have to forego my regular visits to the gym and give up on exercise entirely. But now I have a program that will definitely last a lifetime. And it's a program with a built in advantage; it can easily be adapted for home use. In fact, I suspect many of you won't have to spend an extra penny on exercise equipment to start the Lazy Boy Plus workout. You may not even have to move.

"Avoiding Caffeine?"
The Gazette   May 3, 2004

"Are you sure that's decaf?" I ask for the second time. I can see the server subtly rolling his eyes as he responds affirmatively. 'Of course, it's decaf, you idiot!' he's silently thinking to himself. 'Can't you see the orange ring?'

To those of us over fifty, the question of regular vs. decaf makes a big difference. Like many of my generation (that's the self-indulgent, over-fifty baby boomer crowd for those who were wondering), I've given up on caffeine. This is the latest in my series of denials designed to assist me in living long enough to spend my daughter's inheritance.

I've now had five years of caffeine-free living and, for the most part, it's been a breeze. I experienced few of the withdrawal symptoms suffered by most caffeine addicts. And thanks to the existence of decaffeinated coffee, I've still been able to enjoy the occasional pleasure of the coffee bean without the accompanying risks.

My only dilemma is going out for breakfast. I don't do it often (another denial consistent with the aging process). But when I do, I look forward to the luxury of a full breakfast, a copy of the daily newspaper and a cup of caffeine-free coffee. The problem is I can never be 100% certain that what I'm getting is really decaffeinated.

When I first gave up regular coffee, I frequented a local breakfast spot that had one of the famous orange-ringed coffee pots. Relying on the universal symbol for drug-free coffee, I would indulge myself in a cup with my ham and eggs. But, frequently, I would find that I was a bit edgy and overly alert for the remainder of the day.

Eventually, I discovered that, unlike me, the restaurant proprietor didn't give any special significance to the color orange. If he needed an extra pot for regular coffee, he used the one with the orange ring but continued to pass it off as decaf.

After discovering this cruel deception, I chose to continue eating at the restaurant because the breakfasts were so darned good. My interim solution was to bring along my own cup of decaf to complement the meal.

But after a couple of years of this somewhat awkward and slightly more expensive charade, I decided to take my business elsewhere. A new breakfast eatery opened in my neighborhood with great tasting breakfasts and brewed decaffeinated coffee.

All went well for the first few weeks. Great breakfasts and great tasting decaf. But then it happened. One morning, I had my first cup of decaf and started to feel a bit warm. Cup number two brought on a flushed face and a bit of a headache. Still clueless, I asked for a third cup.

By the time I left the restaurant, I was perspiring like crazy and it felt like someone was playing a game of pinball in my head. By the time I got home, I realized that my caffeine-free body had ingested three cups of regular coffee.

Thanks to that triple dose of "real" coffee, I was in full caffeine-induced agitated mode. So much so that I phoned the restaurant and rapidly and aggressively complained about the injury they had inflicted on me. The hostess assured me that all precautions were taken to ensure that regular and decaffeinated coffee were kept separate. But the buzz in my head suggested otherwise.

After suffering through an overly active day without even the remotest possibility of an afternoon nap, I experienced an epiphany. Most coffee doesn't really taste that great anyway, especially the decaffeinated versions. And since I no longer need a caffeine hit in the morning, I'm going to forego the bean-based beverage altogether. From now on, it's just water for me. That's decaffeinated water, please.

"One Way to Quit Smoking"
The Ottawa Citizen   January 22, 2003

In the words of the old joke, "It's easy to quit smoking; I've done it a hundred times."

How easy is it really? From my perspective, easy as pie. The first time I tried to quit, it worked. Here's how:

For years, I had smoked. Not just social smoking or occasional smoking. I was a real smoker. Two packs a day.

But then in 1984 I decided I had to quit. What was once a pleasurable pastime had become a hard bitten habit.

My clothes and hair stunk of cigarette smoke and my tongue was permanently burnt. I was enjoying maybe two or three of the fifty plus cigarettes I smoked each day.

What finally convinced me to quit was the afternoon fade. Thanks to a daily regimen of progressive carbon monoxide poisoning, by midafternoon I was living in an oxygen-deprived haze.

So I signed up for a local "stop smoking" course. The course effectively combined elements of group therapy, behavior modification and Gestapo torture techniques.

I joined about twenty other nicotine junkies in a biweekly, eight-week program of so-called smoking cessation. Our two instructors were reformed smokers who guided us through the quitting process.

Step one was exploring the mechanism of smoking and identifying our individual smoking patterns. Some people smoked only during the day, some only during the evening and others only when socializing. I, on the other hand, smoked one cigarette every twenty minutes from the time I woke up to the moment I turned off the bedlamp.

Given my hard core status, I didn't seem like a good candidate for quitting. The instructors assumed that I'd been sent there by a spouse or girlfriend and wouldn't last a week. I, too, was beginning to have my doubts.

Step two was to measure the carbon monoxide level of our blood to underscore the deadly nature of our habit. I was the class leader with a CO reading higher than the instructors had ever seen before.

Step three was a challenge. We were to engage in a little

aversion therapy by smoking twice as much for three days. For me, that meant four packs or 100 cigarettes a day. A high goal, yes, but not beyond my smoking capabilities, I thought.

On day one of Gestapo smoking, the CO fade I usually experienced by mid-afternoon showed up mid-morning. By mid-afternoon, I was so spaced out I had to lie down for half an hour. Of course, all that meant was that I had to smoke faster to meet my quota. By day's end, my tongue was on fire and my head was in a fog.

By day two, I was turning green. My body was so full of poisons that I could barely function at work. But I carried on and made it to my Thursday evening session. As I walked in the door, it was clear to the instructors that I was not doing well.

We each had our CO level monitored again, this time to show us how much higher it was after two days of double smoking. In my case, the needle went off the chart. At that point, I told my instructors that I could not carry on for a third day. I had to stop now. They suggested switching to a cigarette brand with a higher tar and nicotine content to allow me to cut back to maybe three packs that final day. I assured them that I could carry on no longer with this double smoking and I presume my ashen face and pitiful tone convinced them.

So I was allowed to proceed immediately to step four: rapid smoking. For the next three days, upon awakening and before eating, I was to smoke three cigarettes rapidly back to back. That meant inhaling every few seconds until I had finished three entire cigarettes.

After that first morning of kamikaze smoking, I was sure that I was going to be sick. Our instructors had warned us to perform this new task in the bathroom, just in case. I now knew why although, by some small miracle, I avoided throwing up.

It might have been better if I had gotten sick. At least that might have diminished somewhat the nausea that I carried with me the rest of the morning. Luckily, I also carried a reminder of that feeling and, like Pavlov's dog, quickly associated it with the act of smoking.

As with step three, I only lasted two days. After a second morning of rapid smoking over the toilet, I could not bear a third. Since my next group meeting was three days away, I boldly decided to throw away my remaining cigarettes and stop completely.

And lo and behold, it took. I didn't smoke that day or the next day or the next. And when I attended the next few meetings, I proudly and amazingly heralded my unbelievable achievement.

At the end of the course, we all vowed to reunite in three months to see how we were doing. To the amazement of the instructors, I proudly showed up with a clean record.

That's not to say I had won the battle. For years after, I still had to fight a rearguard action. Sometimes I would cheat and have two or three cigarettes a day until I would finally rapid smoke one to wean myself again.

On a couple of occasions, I even went back to smoking a pack a day for a week or so. But, as always, my *Clockwork Orange* training eventually clicked in and I would rapid smoke myself back to sobriety.

After many years of mostly smoke-free living, I eventually quit for good. I don't know when that final turning point happened. All I know is that I haven't had a cigarette for years and I can't imagine ever having one again. Especially when I'd have to smoke it in sixty seconds.

"Scratching a 49-year old Itch"
The Ottawa Citizen August 27, 1999

Q: What has 300 spots and whines like a baby?
A: A 49 year old man with chickenpox.

My three year old daughter Sarah recently contracted that common childhood ailment chickenpox. Hers was a typical case. Red spots quickly broke out all over her body and within a few days they started to crust over. In the interim, there were countless baths in oatmeal and baking soda and numerous coatings of calamine lotion. Mom and Dad lost some sleep but after a week the worst was over. Or so we thought.

As Sarah's spots began to disappear, one night I developed a mild fever and a bit of nausea. Even with that, I didn't fully clue in until the next morning when the bathroom mirror revealed a trio of red spots on my forehead.

How could this be? A 49-year-old man with chickenpox? How could I have lived almost half a century and avoided one of the most contagious diseases around?

A trip to my health centre confirmed that I did, in fact, have varicella a.k.a. chickenpox. The nurse-practitioner also informed me that the adult form of the disease was a little nastier than the kid's version.

By the next morning, I had no reason to doubt her prognosis. As my spots multiplied into the dozens and spread to my face and scalp, I began to experience itching - lots of itching. As I lay awake on the sofa at 5 A.M. watching infomercials on TV, I knew this was going to be no ordinary illness.

I spent much of the next day soaking in oatmeal baths and baking soda baths. And when I wasn't in the bathtub, I was standing in front of the mirror dabbing calamine lotion onto the red spots which now numbered in the hundreds. I looked like a giant pincushion.

The next night I pulled out all the stops to ensure that I'd get some sleep. I took a baking soda bath, painted myself with calamine lotion and took two aspirins. To top it off, I downed the remains of my daughter's bottle of Benadryl syrup.

All of that had absolutely no effect. As the itching increased, I again found myself wide awake at five in the morning watching the same commercials for food dehydrators and exercise equipment from the night before.

After unsuccessfully trying a Benadryl-Tylenol cocktail, I called my health centre in desperation. They took pity on me and prescribed another anti-itching medication. I'm not sure it was much better in the anti-itching department than Benadryl, but it also promised to promote drowsiness. Thankfully, it not only promoted drowsiness, it championed out and out unconsciousness. Finally, I was able to sleep.

Thanks to the new medication, I survived the next day and slept through the following night. At last, the worst was over. I assumed that I'd be back to work in a day or two. Alas, it was not to be.

Since it took five days for all of those spots to develop, it took another five days for them to dry up and crust over. By that time, I was happy to get back to the workplace and my wife was even happier. The only ones not as pleased were my co-workers who had to stare at my fading pox marks for the next two weeks.

As my daughter prepares for junior kindergarten in the fall, my excitement is tempered with some trepidation. Who knows what bugs are lurking out there in kiddie land waiting to infect me? People keep telling me that having children keeps you young. But if it also means having mumps at 50, I think I'm ready to be old.

CHAPTER EIGHT

AGING

"A Manly Mid-life Day"
The Ottawa Citizen   February 25, 2002

Wake up at 5 A.M. to urinate for third time. Try to will prostate to shrink.

Lie in bed awake until 6:30 A.M. thinking about mutual fund portfolio and next unsuccessful stock switch. Kick self for not buying Microsoft at 8¼ in 1995. Kick self again for buying it two years ago at 110½.

Get up. Shave. Brush remaining teeth. Consider new application of hair dying gel. Instead convince self that streaks of gray look "distinguished."

Take morning medications. Recall embarrassing incident when morning and evening medications inadvertently switched. Leave sticky note on bathroom mirror as reminder to take evening medications.

Consider going out for traditional ham and eggs breakfast. Remember cholesterol reading and opt instead for "traditional" dry toast and bran flakes breakfast. Sprinkle extra bran powder on cereal for good luck.

Drive to work in leased 1999 Toyota Tercel. Dream of driving Mazda Miata instead. Worry about increased monthly payments when lease is switched to Toyota Echo in 2003.

Take elevator to fifth floor. Smile "coyly" at attractive young woman on elevator. Interpret repulsed frown as subtle flirtation.

Find desk. Turn on computer and read morning paper on-line. Check e-mail and delete all work-related messages. Send replies regarding previously deleted work-related e-mails explaining that you've had hardware and network problems.

Take break. Buy decaf coffee and bran muffin. Take blood pressure reading and consider charting daily bodily functions.

Check investments on-line. Check weather. Check health site by keying in "prostate" and "hypertension." Arrange files for possible work-related activities in afternoon.

Skip lunch. Go to health club and play squash with 32-year old accountant whose knees and hips don't hurt. Lose two games badly. Explain to opponent that your game was "off" and that he made several lucky shots. Dismiss opponent's smile as pathetic attempt to claim legitimate victory.

Shower. Weigh self and record weight on chart. Congratulate self for staying below 210 pounds for sixth straight month. Smugly note that you are "only" 35 pounds and three pants sizes away from college weight.

Return to work. Take elevator to fifth floor. Smile at attractive young woman. Interpret her step backward and premature exit at different floor as subtle sexual signs.

Spot five-dollar bill on floor. Consider picking it up. Reconsider after remembering extended recovery from back injury after carrying garbage pail to curb.

Move work-related files to side of desk. Re-check investments. Re-check weather. Check pharmaceutical site by keying in words "Viagra" and "Celebrex." Wistfully check for possible new drugs under names "Rejuvenex" and "Jung-agin."

Prepare to leave work at 3 P.M. for appointment with rheumatologist. Leave note on message board that you will be late tomorrow due to 9 A.M. appointment with gastroenterologist. Book appointment for next week with cardiologist.

Return home and greet wife and six-year-old daughter. Plan exciting evening with possible outing to view movie at actual cinema. Spouse and self realize outing entails staying up past 10 P.M. Evening plans cancelled.

Eat dinner. Enjoy vegetarian cuisine by fantasizing about 16-oz. steak with baked potato covered in garlic butter. Eat fruit cup for dessert while dreaming of various chocolate confections.

Spouse decides to go out for evening shopping expedition. Inform daughter that you are making "rare" exceptions to no-TV-after-dinner rule and bath-on-Tuesday-night rule. Settle in for 36th viewing of "Little Mermaid II."

As movie ends, daughter nudges you gently. Awake from erotic dream about six-figure portfolio growing to seven figures with annual returns exceeding 25%.

Put daughter to bed. Return to TV and begin watching latest episode of "Frasier." Wake up in time to hear spouse entering front door and see closing credits of TV show.

Dress for bed. Brush remaining teeth and take evening medications. Leave sticky note on bathroom mirror to remind self to take morning medications. Kiss wife goodnight and drift off to sleep.

"Martin v. Father Time"
Stitches Magazine   October, 2002

Since turning fifty, Dave Martin has become litigious. Here is a recent sampling from his crowded court docket:

Martin v. McDonalds, Pizza Hut, et al.
Mr. Martin claims that thirty years of unwitting and inadvertent fat consumption at various fast food chains has resulted in an unexpected gain of six inches to his waist. He is seeking specific damages of $12,500 for additional wardrobe expenses and general damages of $40,000 for loss of ability to see his feet when standing.

Martin v. YMCA
In his statement of claim, Mr. Martin alleges that years of diligent exercise gave him a reasonable expectation of being in good shape. Instead, he now has arthritic hips and knees and has been reduced to riding exercise bicycles. He is looking for $30,000 for medical expenses and loss of enjoyment of squash.

Martin v. Rolling Stones, Led Zeppelin, et al.
The is a class action suit launched by Mr. Martin on behalf of all aging baby boomers who are suffering hearing loss from excessive attendance at 1960s rock concerts. Mr. Martin is hoping for a $500 settlement per class member to cover the cost of a hearing aid, batteries and a Bruce Springsteen Unplugged CD.

Martin v. CBS, NBC and ABC
Mr. Martin is suing the three major American television networks for damages arising from decades of TV viewing. Martin is asking for specific damages of $10,000 to cover the cost of a remedial reading course. He is also seeking punitive damages for declining short term memory and loss of intellect.

Martin v. N.F.L.
Based on the alleged new tort of "weekend warrior enticement", this lawsuit claims that the N.F.L. knew, or ought to have known, that continued viewing of its product would entice Mr. Martin to resume his long dormant touch football career. Martin

wants $5,000 for torn cartilage and a damaged rotator cuff and $10,000 for pain, suffering and loss of ego.

Martin v. The Cattlemen's Association

Always a big beef eater, Mr. Martin is suing cattle ranchers for damages arising from the use of female hormones in cattle feed. Mr. Martin claims this has given rise to a prematurely enlarged prostate and an unwanted collection of oversized lingerie and size 12 pumps. He is seeking damages of $10,000 for nighttime bathroom visits and $25,000 for additional clothing and makeup expenses.

Martin v. Pfizer Inc.

Mr. Martin is suing the makers of Viagra for loss of enjoyment of life. According to his statement of claim, Martin was enjoying the reduced sexual demands of a diminished libido until the advent of Viagra. Now he is expected to perform at a level of a man twenty years his junior. Mr. Martin is seeking damages of $1,000 per sexual encounter or sufficient funds to cover the expenses of a "stand-in."

Martin v. Y Chromosome

Once he can determine a way to effect service of court documents, Mr. Martin intends to sue the Martin family Y chromosome for his male pattern baldness. Damages sought include a toupee and a lifetime membership in the Hair Club for Men.

"My Numbers Are Up"
Stitches Magazine   April, 1997

I recently had to create a secret six-digit code to ensure secure access to my personal computer and it suddenly dawned on me that I had reached numerical overload. A combination of advancing years, advancing technology and declining cranial storage and retrieval abilities had finally caught up with me. No sooner had I created my new computer access code than I had it confused with my voice mail access code, my gym locker combination and my cholesterol count. A quick phone call to a young computer whiz bailed me out but I felt like I had just stepped onto the slippery slope that quickly leads to total innumeracy.

How did I reach this tragic stage so soon? It seemed like only yesterday that I was proudly recalling for anyone who would ask the first number I had committed to memory - my age - which at the time was three and a half. I should have known then that the introduction of the concept of fractions into the life of a child so young did not bode well for my future numerical responsibilities.

But childhood didn't put too much of a strain on my synapses. At some point I committed my birthday to memory and later I was able to recall our home phone number and that of my best friend. Our phone number back then was COlony7-9047 which does nothing more than illustrate that I grew up in the dark ages when phone numbers weren't really phone numbers but rather phone alphanumerics. Still, it was a lot more fun committing BUtterfield8 to memory than some soulless three digit exchange.

About the same time that testosterone first started clouding my brain, I had to memorize my first locker combination and my first bank account number. But despite the hormonal distractions, I was still able to manage these relatively simple tasks.

But before I knew it, I was off to university where I was inundated with a whole series of numbers to remember - everything from a post office box to a student ID number to a library card code. Entering the working world meant even more groups of digits had to be stored for quick retrieval. That social security number I had acquired years before was now being asked for so often that it became etched on my frontal lobe for easy access. Then there were the employee ID numbers, work and home phone numbers, automobile license plate numbers, more bank account numbers and a series of new addresses to alternately learn and forget. The federal government even got into the act and coerced me into committing to memory a zip code or two.

As I advanced in the workplace, my attire changed and I found that there were new numbers that needed ready access. Shirt size, shoe size, jacket size and waist size all had to be put into the storage space atop my neck. And unlike some numbers stored in that space, these ones were variable. Not variable in the sense of changing randomly but variable in the sense of slowly increasing with the passage of time. The memory of 32-inch waist pants is very dim, long since replaced in turn by 34, 36 and 38 with 40 eager to soon step to the front of the line.

Now I'm finding that just as my short and long term memory abilities are starting to decline, advances in technology are accelerating at an increasing rate. And each advance in technology means a new number I have to remember. Without numerical codes, I can't access my computer, my voice mail or my E-mail. And without a PIN (personal identification number) I can't access one of the ubiquitous ATM's (automatic teller machines) which, by the way, illustrates a new challenge - the proliferation of essential acronyms you have to know in order to survive. But that's another story.

As time marches on and I find there are even more numbers to memorize in order to function on this planet ("what's your fax number, sir?"), I fear for my ability to feed and clothe myself. So I'd like to propose a solution to the problem of numerical overload. Everyone should be assigned one number and that number should function to do everything from access your computer to open your gym locker. Imagine - everyone would have his own personal numerical code to serve as his phone number, his license plate number, his fax number and so on.

Since this is my idea, I want to pick my number now before I get stuck with some nine or ten digit creature that I'm likely to forget. Before this concept catches on, I claim the number seven. If I only have to remember a single digit to complete my daily tasks, I figure I should be able to get by well into my fifties. After that, I want a numerical exemption.

"You're Not Getting Older"
Stitches Magazine   January, 2000

As more of us baby boomers pass the half-century mark, there's been a rapid increase in the number of articles and personal essays bemoaning the negative effects of aging. It seems that every boomer who turns fifty feels compelled to publicly wail about his sad fate in facing the inevitable declines in his physical functioning.

'My hair's disappearing.' 'I can't read without glasses.' 'My prostate is swollen.' This ceaseless litany of petty whining can't do much for the image of our generation. We sound as if we're the first ones to ever get old.

Well I, for one, am not going to join the pantheon of pusillanimous crybabies. What's wrong with getting old? Very little.

Consider for a moment the plus side of the aging equation. No more running around trying to impress members of the opposite sex. No more late nights of indulging to excess only to wake up the next morning hung over or worse. And no more fruitless pursuits of something called a "career."

It's time aging boomers awoke to the advantages of advancing years. Look on the bright side of impending death. Here are only seven of the many reasons getting older is definitely better:

(1)   You don't need to worry about arranging medical appointments. By the time you're in your fifties, you've got standing appointments with everyone from your ophthalmologist to your urologist.

(2)   No more constant obsession with sex. Instead of occupying every second thought in your head, now sex is only an occasional topic for consideration.

(3)   It's no longer a problem getting a babysitter for that odd Saturday night out. Since you'll be leaving at 5 P.M. for the early bird special and back by 9, no teenaged baby sitter is going to be inconvenienced since her social life doesn't start until 10.

(4)   It only takes one or two glasses of wine to get a buzz. And three beers is now a party.

(5)   Senior citizen discounts. Even if you haven't turned 55 yet, you probably look it. Take advantage of those wrinkles and ask for reduced prices on everything from movie tickets to prostheses.

(6)   You've got more time on your hands because you have less

hair to comb, fewer teeth to brush and your arms aren't long enough to let you read the newspaper.

(7)   Nobody bugs you. You're getting old and nobody expects anything from you anymore. Let's face it; if someone needs help shovelling the driveway or pushing a stalled car, are they going to ask you or the guy who still walks without a shuffle?

So, come on; stop whining! You're not getting older. Well, actually, you are getting older. But, in many ways, life is also getting easier. Stop complaining and start living. Remember, when life hands you lemons, throw 'em away and order a beer.

"Life After 50"
The Toronto Star   February 25, 2001

    Turning 50 has changed my life and not necessarily for the better. Ever since I entered my sixth decade, declining physical abilities and the medical profession have conspired to monopolize more and more of my time.
    Whereas I used to visit my doctor and dentist once or twice a year, now I seem to have a weekly appointment with one medical practitioner after another. And no longer do I just visit ordinary old GPs. Now I have my own rheumatologist, cardiologist and gastroenterologist.
    All this means that a significant portion of my life is now devoted to having various orifices prodded, explored or filled. Some of these intrusions are minor inconveniences. Others (especially those ending in the letters "oscopy") are not fun at all.
    Last year I was presented with an early Christmas gift in the form of a colonoscopy. Apparently anyone over 50 should have this test, if for no other reason than to let them know that life is short, brutal and painful.
    My test was set for noon on the second Tuesday in December. That meant fasting from Sunday night on, consuming only water, juice, Jell-O and the occasional bowl of consommé. The fast itself wasn't so bad once I got used to it. A liquid diet is almost bearable except for periodic visions of T-bone steaks and apple pies that cloud one's brain.
    But Stage Two is no fun. At 6 the night before the test and 6 the next morning, I had to slowly drink a small bottle of the foulest-tasting laxative ever created. As if that weren't bad enough, the following four hours were filled with continuous, rapid dashes to the bathroom.
    I suspect the pre-test regimen has two purposes: The obvious first one is to clean out your euphemistic system. The not-so-obvious second one is to put you through enough inconvenience and misery that you almost look forward to the test itself.
    If my doctor was looking for a motivated colonoscopy candidate, I was Nobel Prize material. Not only had I suffered through the usual pre-test agony, I was also faced with a snowstorm that (if you'll pardon the expression) dumped a foot of snow on our

street.

Before downing my 6 a.m. laxative cocktail, I spent 45 minutes shovelling out the first six inches of snow from our driveway. Four hours later, I attacked the next six inches, determined to make my 12 o'clock appointment.

Two problems arose. First, the city plows had not yet cleared our street. Second, our telephone was out, the apparent victim of a snow-laden, wind-battered branch bearing down on our outdoor phone line. As my wife went off to use our neighbor's phone to check on the status of my appointment, I climbed to the top of our too short ladder to saw off the offending branch with my 20-year old rusty handsaw. 242 strokes later, the branch broke away. I trudged back into the house to discover that we had a dial tone but I still couldn't dial out.

No phone. No plow. Forty-two hours of fasting and purging. Yet I was undaunted. We all packed into the car and bravely set out down our unplowed street that was buried under a foot of snow. As the car wheels spun and the air filled with the odor of burning rubber and boiling transmission fluid, we slowly advanced to the end of our street. We were almost defeated by the final bend in the road but one final engine-tearing, tachometer-breaking push on the gas pedal launched us forward on to a plowed thoroughfare.

A slow, crawling drive along barely passable streets eventually brought us to the doctor's office. A short wait and, before I knew it, I was lying on a bed with Valium dripping into my left arm and a lighted, flexible probe about to play Star Trek with my intestines.

After all I'd been through, the minor pain and discomfort of the flexible tube exploring my innards was not that bad. I was just relieved that my 42 hours of fasting and voiding were not, so to speak, going to waste. In the end (sorry), I felt pretty good about the whole experience. Then again, it might just have been the Valium.

"Who's On First?"
The Toronto Star   June 19, 2001

Language is our primary means of communication. But given the complexities and intricacies of the English language and our predilection for not listening carefully, we often fail to communicate.

Sometimes that leads to misunderstandings that can affect everything from what we're served for breakfast to the outbreak of war. And on occasion, those misunderstandings lead to laughter.

A classic illustration of the comedic pitfalls in the English language is Abbot and Costello's baseball routine "Who's On First?" What starts out as a simple misapprehension of the contextual meaning of the word "who" leads to a series of hilarious mistakes.

But "Who's On First?" is a comedy routine. It was carefully crafted to extend a linguistic ruse beyond the point of reason. Such an absurd exchange couldn't occur in everyday conversation. Or could it?

Until recently, I figured that there was a limit to real life comedic miscues. It seemed to me that an obvious verbal misunderstanding would become readily apparent in the context of the ongoing conversation. In other words, after a couple of exchanges you'd figure out that the first baseman's name was Who.

On occasion, I'd seen people enter into absurd exchanges but they all ended quickly. And that, I assumed, is how all such conversations ended. Because we are dealing with the responsibilities of everyday life, I thought, absurdity can't survive for more than a couple of mistaken exchanges.

Well, I was wrong and I have the evidence to prove it. Recently I met a fellow in my building at work for the first time and as we were both heading for the elevator I engaged him in conversation about his interests outside the workplace.

"I raise canaries," he said.

That's not what I heard, though. I thought he said that he raced canaries.

"You race canaries?" I said with mild surprise.

"Yes," he said. "A lot of guys in this area raise canaries."

At this point I was struggling to envision what a canary racetrack looked like.

"Do you race them outdoors?" I enquired.

"No, I raise them in my basement," he said.

Still clueless, I tried to make sense of this new piece of information. I pictured a smoke-filled den filled with canary owners betting on the outcome of the next race.

"Do you use an enclosed track?" I asked in all sincerity, assuming that you couldn't train canaries to independently fly in an oval path.

"Yes, I have wire cages," he said which made perfect sense if you raise canaries rather than race them.

I, on the other hand, pictured a giant, enclosed, wire-mesh, oval track suspended from his basement ceiling. I also pictured a whole subculture of canary racers much in the fashion of dogsled owners. If people can race dogs or even pigeons, I reasoned, why not canaries?

The elevator stopped at my floor and I got off, my head still reeling with visions of the third race at the canary equivalent to Churchill Downs. A co-worker who witnessed the entire exchange with glee clued me in to my mistake and brought me back to reality.

"Racing canaries" made a great tale for a couple of days. But after awhile, I started wondering. If I hadn't gotten off that elevator, how much longer would our conversation in parallel universes have gone on? Was there a limit? How far into canary racing wonderland would I have descended? Unfortunately, like Abbot and Costello's third baseman, "I Don't Know."

"Are You There God?"
The Ottawa Citizen   July 9, 2005

MEMORANDUM
TO: God
FROM: Dave

      Thanks again for the last 54 years. For the most part, it's been great fun. But looking back over the past five decades, there are a few minor suggestions I'd like to make for your next re-design of the male body:
1.   Try to keep the hair distribution even. Having the hair loss on the top of the head offset by a commensurate growth on the ears and upper back seems a bit wasteful. Why not let us just keep the hair on our head for life?
2.   How about making our teeth out of something a little sturdier? I've noticed that the last two put in by my dentist are made out of gold and seem to be holding up very well. Why not start us out with a mouthful of metal choppers and save us the pain and expense of a lifetime of dentist visits?
3.   Please don't let our chest slide into our belly. It's bad enough that we have to put on extra weight as we age without having to buy a new wardrobe every two or three years as well.
4.   Looking back, it would have been nice to have the lifetime supply of testosterone regulated. How come we're given so much at age 18 that we can't think straight but are shortchanged at 58? Just even out the supply, please.
5.   While we're on the subject of sex, please re-think the prostate gland. It serves a useful function, no doubt, but why have it encircling the urethra? After all, it would be nice to rely on something other than gravity to relieve oneself after age 60.
6.   Was it really necessary to have the eyes change after 40? It's not like I can't adjust to bifocals, trifocals or whatever's coming next. But it seems to me that it would be easier just to keep them functioning at one level throughout.
7.   Oh, yes, and before I forget (which I've been doing more and more often, of late), how about increasing our memory? If they can add a gig or two to my PC, why can't you do it for the male brain, too?

8.   Finally, without accusing you of sexism or the like, it would be nice if you could give us some of those neat extras women get. I'm not talking about breasts or softer skin or even the ability to talk about our feelings. All we'd really like is that multiple orgasm thing. Either that, or let us be 18 again.

CHAPTER NINE

DARE TO BE AVERAGE

"Dare to be Average"
Stitches Magazine   November, 1997

Are you depressed, unhappy, unfilled? Have you often wondered what your life would be like if only you could unload all your worries and neuroses? Have you ever wanted to be more than you are?

Of course you have. And why? Because you've been subjected to a never ending onslaught of newspaper ads, junk mail and infomercials telling you how to overcome your boring humdrum life by doing everything from losing thirty pounds to getting buns of steel to buying real estate with no money down.

Everyone from Anthony Robbins to Charles Givens has assaulted you with entreaties whose underlying message is "I'm OK; you're so-so" and whose upfront message is "Send me $200 and I'll make everything okay." You can't turn on the TV today without one of these motivational gurus urging you to change your life.

Well, I'm here to tell you that your life is alright just the way it is. You don't need to lose thirty pounds, you don't need a fancy new car and you sure don't need more "personal power", whatever the hell that is.

You need an antidote to the pop psych, simplistic aphorisms of Messrs. Robbins, et al. The answer? Just follow my easy six-step program "Dare to be Average."

I'm offering my six-step program to anyone who can read this page. It's a simple inaction plan for those who don't want to get ahead or expand their horizons or lose any weight. In other words, it's a way for us everyday slobs to get on with our lives and enjoy the occasional relaxing break we get when the hyped-up motivational wizards can't get at us.

My "message for the mediocre" is really quite simple: don't change, you're fine just the way you are. And here's my simple six-step program to ensure that you continue to meet that goal:

(1) Stop worrying about getting rich; wealth only creates a whole new series of problems. What would you do with ten million dollars anyway? You'd have to hire a lawyer, an accountant and a personal bodyguard and you'd no longer be able to enjoy anonymity. Life would become a series of one financial headache after another. So, if you have any excess cash, just stick it in the bank and forget about it.

(2)   Stop worrying about "personal growth"; it's highly overrated. What's wrong with laying back, reading, watching TV or just lazing the day away? Nothing, of course. The only reason you've been feeling guilty about it at all is because Anthony Robbins and his gang have made you feel that way. Well, forget it. It's time to get back on that sofa and enjoy those *Mash* reruns guilt-free.

(3)   Stop worrying about diet and health. What's the point? In the last ten years we've been told margarine's good for us and then we're told it's bad for us. Alcohol was bad for us; now it's good. Oat bran was a miracle cure; now it's suspect. Regular coffee was out; decaf was in. But now decaf is supposedly worse than regular. If you had just stuck to your old meat and potatoes diet from ten years ago, you'd be better off today and you wouldn't have suffered through the stress and worry of trying to keep up with the *New England Journal of Medicine*.

(4)   Stop worrying about fitness and exercise. Let's face it - no one ever sprained an ankle in a rocker-recliner. So, throw out that fancy exercise equipment that Jane or Jake or some other TV personality sold you for three easy payments of $39 and enjoy living again. If you leave that portable gym in the corner of the rec room, you're just going to feel guilty and inadequate every time you look at it. So chuck it out and ensure that the toughest exercise you ever engage in again is operating the remote control.

(5)   Stop getting sucked in to buying every new glitzy device hawked on the tube. Believe it or not, you don't need a power walker or a food dehydrator or a ginzu knife set. Before phoning that 1-800 number or sending in a cheque for $79.95, stop and think where that convection cooker is going to end up. Right next to the two dozen other gizmos that you thought you couldn't do without but now gather dust in the corner of the basement. Just remember, when's the last time you used the Pocket Fisherman, the Vegematic or the Pattystacker that you bought twenty years ago?

(6)   Stop worrying about getting old. It happens to everyone and you can't avoid it. We age, our hair falls out, our skin wrinkles and we eventually die. That's life. Save your money and stop believing the infomercial wizards trying to sell you the fountain of youth. For women, that means stop buying the infinite variety of anti-wrinkle skin creams. For men, it means no more purchases of toupees, hair weaves or hair plugs; it's a lot cheaper to just buy a hat.

Now you're probably saying to yourself "Hey, this guy's right - I don't need to buy all those things - but how do I buy a copy of his amazing new videotape?" You don't. That's the whole idea. No more exercise videos, no more dieting infomercials and no more personal growth audiocassettes. You don't need them.

So don't send me any money, don't call my 1-800 number and please don't write me. I don't want to be bothered. I've got better things not to do.

"Seven Habits of Unmotivated People"
The Toronto Star   February 13, 1998

For years now, you've been assaulted with one self-help book after another. From Anthony Robbins' "Dare to be Great" to Stephen Covey's "The Seven Habits of Highly Successful People", the message is the same: you're not doing so hot and here's how you can do better.

And if it isn't a self-help book, it's an infomercial or a self-improvement videotape. Everyone from Jane Fonda to Charles Givens has harassed you with entreaties whose underlying message is "I'm OK; you're so-so" and whose upfront message is "Send me $29.95 and I'll make everything okay." You can't turn on the TV today without one of these motivational gurus urging you to change your life.

Well, I'm here to tell you that your life is alright just the way it is. You don't need to lose thirty pounds, you don't need abs of steel and you sure don't need more "personal power", whatever the hell that is. What you do need is to dare to be average.

Let's face it; most of us have no desire to do better. Doing better involves a lot of effort and hard work. What us average folks are looking for is a simple way to maximize sofa time, TV time and nap time.

If I were ambitious, I'd sit down and write a book detailing the lazy life and how you can achieve it. But I have no more desire to break a sweat than you do. That's why the best I could do is this short essay listing a few handy hints to make life a little more bearable. Even at that, it took me two years to get around to writing this piece.

What follows is a compilation of invaluable advice garnered from people who have become highly proficient in leading the average life and doing as little as possible. I'd like to tell you that I spent months travelling from coast to coast interviewing dozens of these folks but that would be a lie. Plus, it would have violated the whole purpose of this essay - avoiding work.

What I did do was to phone a few friends whose butts are permanently attached to La-Z-Boy chairs and asked them their secrets for achieving that state of grace. From an extensive list of ten guidelines and lifestyle hints, I whittled it down to seven. I proudly present them to you now, the seven habits of highly unmotivated people:

(1)   Don't buy clothes with buttons. T-shirts and sweat pants are ideal. If you have to buy something that can't be pulled on, make sure it has a zipper.
(2)   Don't buy shoes with laces. Loafers, slippers and deck shoes are the best. If you absolutely need a tighter fit, buy something with Velcro straps.
(3)   Always buy prepared, ready-to-eat food. If you must buy something requiring preparation, make sure it fits in the microwave. Never use a regular oven except when the furnace breaks down.
(4)   Economize and save where you can but do not scrimp on your TV remote control. Always buy the best and keep extra batteries in the arm of your rocker-recliner.
(5)   Replace your lawn with Astroturf or wood chips and cut down any leaf-bearing trees.
(6)   Don't replace things until they break and then buy used. Don't repair items; life's too short.
(7)   Don't answer the phone or your doorbell and never open your mail.

"Seven Steps to Average"
Stitches Magazine   November, 1999

     In this age of self-improvement and over achievement, we've been inundated with books, tapes and videos telling us how to improve everything from our job to our diet. Well, enough is enough. It's time to tell the motivational experts to take a hike and get back to living the average life.

     For many of you, it won't be difficult to "dare to be average." Every fiber of your being cries out: "Lie down on that sofa and eat those potato chips."

     But for some of you, living the average life won't come easily. You've read so many self-improvement books and followed so many self-actualization plans that you've lost touch with your inner slob.

     So if you're stuck in a self-help rut and can't seem to get out, you may need to follow my new "Dare To Be Average Workout Plan." It's a seven-step daily regimen that can quickly lead to a slower, larger, lazier you.

<u>STEP ONE:</u>   Stop setting your alarm clock. The early bird may get the worm but, trust me, worms don't taste very good. You'll be much better off with a couple of more hours of sleep.

<u>STEP TWO:</u>   Do not comb your hair, put on makeup or shave. Do you realize that if you spend fifteen minutes a day on personal grooming that over a lifetime that adds up to many minutes? And however many minutes it is, that's time better spent doing nothing.

<u>STEP THREE:</u>   Resist the urge to read the newspaper. You don't need to know what's going on in the world; it'll only depress you. If you have to get some hard news, just watch *Entertainment Tonight*.

<u>STEP FOUR:</u>   Watch TV. If you've been "off the tube" for awhile, it may take some time to wean you back on. In the first week, restrict yourself to no more than an hour a day of something highbrow like <u>Masterpiece Theatre</u>. Over the next few weeks slowly include a few mainstream programs. By week six you can safely add sitcoms and game shows. By week ten you should be able to easily handle a whole day of talk shows and soaps.

<u>STEP FIVE:</u>   Change your diet. Again, don't make a quick radical change; ease yourself into a balanced lifestyle. Each week, substitute a high fat or high sugar food item for one of those so-called healthy choices foisted on you by the diet gurus. Week one: substitute bacon

and eggs for bran flakes. Week two: eliminate green vegetables; add fried anything. Week three: dump the rice cakes; add real cake. By week ten you should be able to eat just about anything you want.

STEP SIX: Can the exercise. This one doesn't have to be gradual. Just stop working out - now! You'll start feeling better right away.

STEP SEVEN: Dump the aphorisms. If you've been following all those self-improvement programs, your mind is probably polluted with catchy phrases like "Awaken The Giant Within" or "If You Can Dream It, You Can Do It." Let go of the slogans and watch your mind atrophy overnight. If you have trouble with this one, just replace all those clever sayings with your new mantra: "Dare To Be Average."

Those are your seven steps to a new sedentary lifestyle. It looks like a challenging program but, believe me, it's not. In a matter of weeks, you'll be able to experience a new heavier, happier you. With your weight and heart rate up by 25% and your activity level cut in half, you'll be well on your way to being average.

"I'd Like to Volunteer"
The Toronto Star   August 20, 1998

The latest results are in. Drinking red wine is definitely good for your heart. A recent British study has confirmed that drinking half a bottle of cabernet sauvignon a day helps to keep the arteries unclogged. A control group drinking a lemon soda concoction with ten per cent vodka failed to achieve the same benefits.

I'm pleased to hear this news. As a red wine drinker, I now have a rationalization for consuming that half bottle of vino with dinner.

What I'd really like, of course, is to be a participant in one of these studies. If some white-coated, lab guys need someone to down a daily half bottle of red wine, I'm their guy. In fact, I probably wouldn't even mind being one of those vodka-swilling members of the control group.

And if there are more studies in the works, I'd like to get in on them, too. For example, if some researcher is designing a study to investigate the effects of meaningless sex with blond supermodels, I'd be pleased to volunteer.

I can also help out in other scientific investigations. I'd be more than happy to join any study that wanted to explore the effects of eating pie and ice cream on a regular basis. Naturally, a five year study would be preferred.

The long term consequences of not working is another area that sorely needs further investigation. Although I would have to give up my job to participate, I'd be willing to pursue the leisure life for as long as it takes. If it's in the interests of science, no sacrifice is too great.

This leads me to another possible protocol for examination - early retirement. Again, I'm ready to help out.

Any kind of sleep study would get my participation. The effects of overuse of the television remote control is also right up my alley. And I'm not averse to being a subject for any number of drug interaction tests.

Finally, I think it's time that researchers tailored their studies to the needs and desires of specific segments of the population. In my case, I'd like to participate in an extended investigation of the effects of sports car ownership on the libido of aging males.

Now, I don't mean to suggest that I'm willing to be a guinea pig for any old study that comes along. There are some research projects that I have no desire to join.

Like the investigation of the long term effects of excessive coffee consumption. Been there; done that. Or anything involving injections or lab rats. I have my limits.

There are other areas of scientific research I'd rather avoid. A study of the gastrointestinal effects of a high fiber diet? No thanks. An investigation of the lifestyle changes incurred by TV deprivation? Not for me.

And I have absolutely no interest in being the subject of a look into the health benefits of a vegetarian diet. I'll leave that one to more dedicated souls.

Hopefully, I'll get to be a participant in one of my studies of choice. And once I do, I'm sure that researchers will recognize my unique traits and sign me up for even more investigations. In time, I'm hoping to be able to drive my red sports car to my favorite restaurant to eat red meat washed down with red wine. And all in the name of science.

"You Have One Minute, 28 Seconds"
The Toronto Star   September 9, 1998

Have you noticed the recent fashion for using the designation "anal-retentive" in a pejorative sense? I didn't think so. Well, that's probably because you're not an anal-retentive. But I am and I'm miffed.

A computer search of major daily newspapers revealed exactly seven articles containing derogatory references to that term. In those articles, anal-retentives have been condemned as people who utter banalities, obsessively maintain perfect lawns and exhibit rigid behavior in the extreme. We've even been accused of overflossing, as if that's possible!

Enough is enough. It's time for us anal-retentives to unite and fight this slanderous calumny.

Where would the world be without the careful attentions of the anal-retentive personality? It would be in one sorry, unruly, ungodly mess, that's where.

Anal-retentives keep the world in order. We take out the garbage, clean up the messes and straighten the pictures on the wall.

We make sure things start on time (or even early, if possible). We insist on orderly and fair queuing wherever lineups form (or ought to form). And we never, ever wear mismatched socks.

In short, we are the guardians of Western civilization. And what do we get for our troubles? Abuse, disrespect and ridicule.

Well, no more. It's time for anal-retentives everywhere to come out of their well-organized closets and stand up for their rights. It's time to organize not just our desks but ourselves. Let's join together and claim our rightful place as the non-toxic, washable glue that holds society together.

If you'd like to join me in this noble endeavor, please send in an application form neatly completed (in pen, please!) on a 8½ x 11 single-spaced sheet of white paper. But before you put pen (preferably fountain) to paper (preferably bond), you might want to take the following test to see if you qualify for membership in my National Establishment of Anal-retentive Types (N.E.A.T.). Give yourself one point for each positive response.

(1)   You've never incurred a late charge at the video store.
(2)   The bills in your wallet or purse are sorted by denomination.

(Give yourself a bonus point if they're all facing the same way.)

(3)   Yellow sticky notes on memos and files must be straight. Hey - I said straight! You call that straight?

(4)   You've never paid interest charges on a credit card bill.

(5)   Your chequebook balances every month.

(6)   You've never found it amusing when it's said of Mussolini that at least he made the trains run on time.

(7)   You never squeeze the toothpaste in the center of the tube. I mean never. Hey - what are you doing? Put that cap back on!

(8)   The CDS in your record collection (and the LPS in the basement) are arranged alphabetically by artist. (Give yourself an extra point if they're cross-referenced by album title.)

Finally, if you even bothered to take this quiz, give yourself two bonus points. Then tally up your score. If you checked the total more than once, take another bonus point.

If you scored more than five, welcome aboard. If you scored more than ten, you qualify for a lifetime membership. As for the rest of you - watch out. N.E.A.T. is on the rise!

"Recycling for Dummies"
The Ottawa Citizen   March 20, 2000

The Regional-Municipality of Urban-Decay and the Townships of Hither, Thither and Yon are pleased to announce the further expansion of our award-winning Recycling Program. In response to your requests for a simpler, more efficient system, we've updated the Program to serve you better.

Effective September 1st, please note the following changes:

(1) Your blue box will now be reserved solely for cans and packaging made from metals with an atomic number less than or equal to 26. Don't forget to wash the items thoroughly and crush to a thickness of no more than one inch. For larger items, call our special Cancycle pickup service at 555-1636. Don't forget to ask for the free plastic gauge with the one-inch slot to help you sort your blue box items.

(2) The black box remains the primary receptacle for paper products except for cardboard. Under the new program, no more sorting by paper type. Fine paper, wrapping paper, flyers and newspapers can all go in your black box. We would, however, ask you not to include copies of *The Star* or *The National Enquirer*. Please bundle these separately and call 555-1637 for special nighttime pickup.

(3) The green box has changed function to more accurately reflect its primary color. Starting September 1st, the green box is no longer to be used for clear glass bottles and small auto parts. Instead, use it for leaves, plants, lawn clippings and other yard-related organic waste. Please do *not* include animal products or body parts of any type. The municipal composter cannot handle such items. Please dispose of them through your regular refuse collection or call the police at 555-1777.

(4) We've added the red box this year to make recycling even easier. The red box is exclusively for plastic containers regardless of the code imprinted on the bottom. All plastic recyclables can be included so long as the caps and labels have been removed, they've been washed and thoroughly dried and they've been crushed to a thickness of one inch or less. What could be simpler? Don't forget - you can use your plastic gauge from the blue box to make sorting a snap.

(5) We've also added the yellow box to handle miscellaneous recyclables. This is the one to use for Styrofoam containers, glass bottles, aluminum foil, milk cartons and those not quite plastic - not quite cardboard thingies used for microwave dinners. If you have trouble keeping track of what goes in the yellow box, just remember the handy acronym SGAM².

Municipal workers will be distributing the new red and yellow boxes commencing the first week of August. If you order now, they will also deliver a handy six-shelf plastic shed to store your boxes. It's only $50 and it comes in your choice of slate gray, army green or puce. Call 555-1638 and have your credit card handy.

In conjunction with the new yellow and red boxes, we've also changed the pickup schedule to make the system even more user-friendly. Starting September 1st, you'll no longer have to remember what zone you live in to determine which day to put out your recyclables. Now the entire Urban-Decay region will follow the same plan.

Put out your blue box on Monday and your black box on Tuesday. Wednesday is green box day, Thursday is red box day and the yellow box goes out on Friday. For holiday weekends, just move each box up a day and double up the yellow box and the blue box on the following Monday.

Regular refuse collection will still be on your designated day depending on your residence zone. Please consult the booklet "When Do I Put Out My Damn Garbage?" to determine the day and time to take your garbage to the curb.

We're proud of the changes to our Recycling Program. You've spoken out and we've listened to your complaints and suggestions. We've taken your threats of legal action to heart and designed a system that we think is second to none. To help with the transition, we've added a Recycle Hotline (555-1639). Please feel free to call and leave a message anytime.

Enjoy the ease and convenience of the new Recycling Program. And look for the newly upgraded Leaf Program coming this fall. Your instructional video, bag maker and regional leaf map should be in the mail soon. Remember - together we can make a difference!

"Could You Leave Me a Note?"
The Chicago Tribune   April 2, 2002

I'm losing faith in mankind. Nobody writes anymore.

I'm not talking about letters. I've long given up on the possibility of engaging in postal exchanges of thoughtful correspondence. Like most, I've accepted reality and confined my missives to e-mail.

No, I'm mourning the loss of the note left on your windshield by the person who accidentally dings your car. Once these notes were as common as parking lot accidents, or so I've been told.

In the golden age of honesty, apparently drivers would almost always leave a note. Nothing fancy, mind you. Just something to express regret for the accident and to provide a name, phone number and insurance information.

Given my recent experience, I'm a bit sceptical about these tales of widespread honesty. I'm beginning to think the so-called "windshield note" is just a figment of a nostalgic imagination Personally, I've never received one.

Three years ago, someone backed into my brand new Toyota Tercel. With a $300 deductible on my car insurance, I was on the hook for the $310 repair bill. Plus I lost my car for two days. And no note.

One year ago, someone hit my wife's Mazda in a community center parking lot. Bumper and parking light repairs totalled $907 and we ate the $300 deductible. No note.

Two months ago, the Mazda was parked on a quiet street while my wife escorted my daughter to school. Within minutes, someone drove by and demolished the side view mirror. $285, more inconvenience and, of course, no note.

Last month, I made the mistake of leaving my car in a shopping center parking lot for thirty minutes. Vulnerable to careless drivers, my poor little Tercel suffered a broken taillight. $225 in repairs and still no note.

I'm less concerned with the fact that each of these four incidents was a hit-and-run accident, a serious offense under any highway traffic statute. I'm more concerned with the apparent skyrocketing illiteracy rate among modern drivers. I'm most concerned with the increasing lack of honesty and civility in society.

So what's the solution? More money for education? Better parenting skills to help impart minimal ethical standards? Squads of parking lot vigilantes to hunt down violators? Exploding paint that sprays offending vehicles on impact?

I don't know. But I do know that if someone doesn't write me a note soon, I'm going to throw away my pen.

"A Membership Drive for the Latter Day Daves" The Chicago Tribune May 22, 2002

It's been a tough year for the world's major religions. The Catholic Church has been rocked by sex scandals. Islam has been hijacked by fundamentalist extremists. The Jewish faith is under attack in Israel and Hindus are at odds with Muslims and Sikhs. Even Buddhists are feeling the heat.

In the interests of providing some theological relief, I'm inviting one and all to join the Modern Church of Latter Day Daves. Although originally formed as a low maintenance faith for Daves of limited ambition, I figure it's time to open this religion to everybody.

With no elaborate rituals and no messy history, we Latter Day Daves try to take the work out of religion. You don't need a credo. You don't need a prayer book. Why, you don't even need to believe in God.

We have no leader, no hierarchy and no complicated rules. It's a no pressure faith. And, apart from NFL football, we have no Sunday services.

All we ask is that you follow our basic ten commandments:
1) Rotate your tires.
2) Maintain your barbecue.
3) Buy the biggest TV set you can afford.
4) Always have a spare remote control or at least some extra batteries.
5) Don't attempt electrical repairs.
6) Don't attempt plumbing repairs.
7) Hire someone to do your snow removal.
8) Do not change the oil in your car. Let someone else do it.
9) Dandelions are sacred. Do not remove them from your lawn.
10) Our sacrament is wine but beer is OK, too.

But don't worry. If you break the odd commandment, no one's going to care. They're really more like guidelines.

Now you're probably saying to yourself: "How do I join this great religion?" Well, all you have to do is grab a beer from the fridge, lie down on the sofa, turn on the TV and say three times: "It's great to be Dave. It's great to be Dave. It's great to be Dave."

Welcome aboard.

"A Night Out at the Movies"
The Ottawa Citizen   December 14, 2002

Thank you unnamed Giant Movie Chain for providing me another evening of cinematic entertainment. It had been awhile since I had enjoyed the experience of watching a first run movie on a big screen. So when my wife suggested (or, to be more accurate, insisted) that we actually go out to see a film, I was unsure of what to expect.

Well, let me be the first to congratulate you. Not only did you meet most of my expectations, you exceeded many of them. And then some.

I expected the tickets to be pricey, of course. Score one for you. Two tickets cost us $24. By my calculation, I could rent five fairly current films for that amount and still have enough left over for a box of microwave popcorn.

Which brings me to your refreshment offerings. For one bag of popcorn and two drinks, I forked out another $12. And this wasn't for your supersized buckets and barrels. This was just for an ordinary bag of popcorn and two 12-ounce drinks.

Luckily, we arrived early since our chosen film was playing in one of your eight "theaters" that had only sixty seats. Historically, I was used to cinemas with seating for hundreds, not dozens. In the previous century, this was a common feature of movie houses since it helped accommodate the giant movie screen.

Now here's where you let me down a bit. I had hoped that for our $36 expenditure we would get to see our movie on a big screen. You know, one that is measured in yards rather than inches.

I never dreamed that we would have gone to all this trouble to watch a movie on a glorified TV screen. Granted, it was bigger than our home TV. But that's only because we can't yet afford one of the new 96" home theaters. If we could, then I'm not sure there would be much reason to patronize your facility anymore. Except perhaps to experience your sound system.

Here, you again exceeded my expectations. You have a very powerful sound system and you're not afraid to use it. In fact, I can still hear it ringing in my ears two days later.

I can only surmise that, for whatever reason, you have decided that the sound level should be inversely proportional to the size of the screen. Perhaps it's a question of overcompensation. Or perhaps having challenged our vision, you wished to also test the limits of our hearing.

And once we had met those challenges, it was apparent that you also wanted to test our patience. I speak here of the previews of so-called "coming attractions." I'm always game for one or two of these, if for no other reason than to take note of what future movies to steer clear of.

Again, you exceeded my expectations. I lost count of the previews after number five, shortly after the ringing in my ears began. A ringing undoubtedly precipitated by the 120 decibel basso profundo voiceover that accompanied each preview.

Did I mention the lovely surprise you threw in before the previews? Presumably to make us feel at home, the previews were preceded by commercials, just like we see at home on our own TV. I was inclined to complain but, as my wife so rightly pointed out, they were top quality commercials. Presumably the kind that you spend good money to see in a movie theater.

Oh yes, the movie. It seemed a bit anticlimactic after all that but it was an enjoyable film. And I suspect that I enjoyed it almost as much as if I had waited a few months to rent it at my local video store for $4.

Then again, if I had waited to view it at home, I would have missed out on the social aspect of communal movie watching. That would have meant foregoing the tall man with bushy hair partially blocking my view of the "giant" screen. Or passing up the opportunity to listen in on the intriguing tale of the gall bladder operation of the woman behind me. Or missing out on the subtle fragrances of half a dozen people apparently wealthy enough to bathe in perfume.

Once my wife and I had finally exited the unnamed Giant Movie Chain and headed home, I began to have doubts about this experience called "a night out" at the movies. Tallying up the $6 parking charge and the $20 babysitting fee, I calculated our night out cost us $62.

My wife feels that we should engage in this activity at least once a month. I, on the other hand, plan to do some research at my local TV superstore. For a $62 monthly payment, I'm pretty sure we can get a "home theater" almost as big as yours. And, guess what, the sound level is adjustable.

"Dave's Law"
Stitches Magazine   February, 2003

In today's modern democracy, the legislative process is increasingly controlled by the lobbying efforts of various special interest groups. Automobile and airplane manufacturers get government grants, farmers get subsidies and drug companies get extended patent protection. Accordingly, I intend to protect my own special interests and lobby Parliament to pass what I hope will become *An Act respecting Dave*, Statutes of Canada 2002, chapter C-555.

Section 1
This Act may be cited as *Dave's Law*.
Section 2 - Applicability to all Daves
The provisions of this chapter shall apply to all Daves irrespective of province of residence and notwithstanding possible contrary provisions in the laws or ordinances of any province, territory or municipality.
Section 3 - Highway traffic laws exemption
All Daves are exempt from the application of any laws, regulations or by-laws governing the ownership or operation of a motor vehicle. Without limiting the generality of the foregoing, Daves can borrow anyone else's vehicle, go as fast as they want and park anywhere they damn well please.
Section 4 - Voluntary payment of taxes
The payment of all federal, provincial, municipal, property, sales and excise taxes by Daves is purely voluntary. Daves may pay whatever they choose to the appropriate taxing authority and are free to tell Revenue Canada to effect a self-placement in a location devoid of solar rays.
Section 5 - Preferential treatment for dining, social and sporting events
Daves are not required to stand in line for tickets for any sporting, musical or theatrical event and are deemed to have reservations for the time, date and restaurant of their choice. Daves have an unfettered "cut in" privilege for any line-up anywhere.

Section 6 - Home entertainment privileges

Daves shall have care and control of the primary home television receiver and associated recording devices (see Schedule I: VCR and DVD regulations). Ownership and operation of any available remote control device shall be exclusive to Daves.

Section 7 - Dietary guidelines

No Dave shall be required to eat any unfried vegetable product or any food having a French name. The "Dave food groups" are henceforth designated as red meat, red wine, fried goods and baked goods.

Section 8 - Clothing requirements

Daves may wear any clothing they wish subject only to regional modesty standards (see applicable local regulations re: Speedo bathing suits and Spandex bicycle shorts). No Dave can be forced to discard used underwear, chinos or T-shirts unless the number of tears, rips or holes exceeds his age.

Section 9 - Gardening responsibilities

Daves are required to maintain and mow both the front and back lawn. Weed removal shall be conducted on a "best efforts" basis. No Dave shall be required to plant, water, weed or otherwise maintain any flower (perennial or annual), vegetable (root or leafy) or bush (dead or alive).

Section 10 - Barbecue exclusivity

Daves shall have exclusive domain over the outdoor gas barbecue and all associated accessories including, but not limited to, the tongs, the spatula, the rotating spit and the automatic starter. Daves may relinquish temporary control of the barbecue for the cooking or broiling of fish and/or vegetables.

Section 11 - Penalties

Whoever knowingly violates any of the foregoing provisions is guilty of a summary offense and is subject to a fine of not less than ten dollars and a severe personal reprimand from Dave.